EARLY CHILDHOOD EDUCATION

YESTERDAY, TODAY, AND TOMORROW

EARLY CHILDHOOD EDUCATION
YESTERDAY, TODAY, AND TOMORROW

SUZANNE L. KROGH
KRISTINE L. SLENTZ
WESTERN WASHINGTON UNIVERSITY

 LAWRENCE ERLBAUM ASSOCIATES, PUBLISHERS

2001 MAHWAH, NEW JERSEY   LONDON

Lawrence Erlbaum Associates, Inc., Publishers
10 Industrial Avenue
Mahwah, New Jersey 07430

Cover design by Kathryn Houghtaling Lacey

Library of Congress Cataloging-in-Publication Data

Krogh, Suzanne.
    Early childhood education : yesterday, today, and tomorrow / by Suzanne L. Krogh and
Kristine L. Slentz.
        p.   cm.
    Includes bibliographical references (p.) and index.
    ISBN 0-8058-2882-6 (pbk. : alk. paper)
    1. Early childhood education—United States.   I. Slentz, Kristine.   II. Title.

LB1139.25 .K75 2001
372.21′0973   00-023249
                                                                                     CIP

Books published by Lawrence Erlbaum Associates are printed on acid-free paper,
and their bindings are chosen for strength and durability.

Printed in the United States of America
10 9 8 7 6 5 4 3 2 1

To our families, friends, and colleagues who supported and motivated us, and tolerated our occasional preoccupation—you know who you are

CONTENTS

TO OUR READERS AND THEIR INSTRUCTORS: AN INTRODUCTION TO THE SERIES

The book you are now beginning is one of a series of four interrelated texts. Taken together, they provide an introduction to the broad field of early childhood education. Usually, such introductions are provided to students in one large survey textbook. Over the years, however, our knowledge of early development as it relates to education has increased enormously at the same time that legislative and cultural issues have grown in number. Add to that the fact that more and more early childhood centers and classrooms include youngsters who would once have been segregated in self-contained special education classes and it becomes evident that now all teachers of young children need to understand development and education across a broad spectrum of abilities. We thus are faced with a problem: Introductory textbooks must either get much longer and heavier, or simply skate across the surface of their topics.

Meanwhile, college and university instructors must decide how to fit this expanded knowledge and information into their courses. The answers they arrive at are many and various, making the traditional all-purpose textbook a source of frustration for many.

This series of textbooks has been designed to alleviate the frustration by offering four modules divided by general subject areas:

- an overview of history and the current field of early education;
- typical and atypical growth and development, infancy through the third grade;
- models and methods of teaching and guiding behavior; and
- curriculum, with a focus on preschool and the primary grades.

By creating this modular scheme, we have been able to treat each topic in more depth and incorporate discussions of abilities and needs across all levels, including developmental delays and giftedness. Instructors are invited to mix and match the texts as appropriate to their own interests and needs.

The titles of the four books in the series are:

Volume I: Early Childhood Education: Yesterday, Today, and Tomorrow
Volume II: Early Childhood Development and Its Variations
Volume III: Teaching Young Children
Volume IV: The Early Childhood Curriculum

We hope you find this new approach to early childhood courses a useful and refreshing one. We welcome your feedback and ideas.

—Suzanne Krogh   —Kristine Slentz
  Elementary Education   Special Education
  Western Washington University   Western Washington University
  Suzanne.Krogh@wwu.edu   Kristine.Slentz@wwu.edu

PREFACE

This book is designed to be the first in a series for early childhood education. It contains chapters on topics that are typically and traditionally regarded as foundational to other, later learning. Foundational topics ask us to think, reflect, and develop opinions, theories, and philosophies. Rarely do they directly answer that basic question of survival, "What will I do Monday morning?!"

Topics that cause us to reflect, however, have a long-term utility that supports us far beyond next Monday. They help us understand why we think the way we do about our methods of teaching, the materials we select, and our expectations for children. So, when we have run out of activities in all our practical activity books, we aren't left high and dry wondering what to do next. Because we have developed a solid philosophy and understand why we do what we do, we can begin to create plans that support children's growth in all the best ways. And, when we explore more of those activity books, we know how to choose the very best experiences.

Occasionally, a college instructor might choose to reverse the order of presentation of the books in this series and save the foundational book for last. Beginning teachers thus have the opportunity of first gaining experience with children, collecting some practical ideas from veteran teachers, and thinking about curriculum ideas right from the beginning. They can think about Monday with an emerging sense of confidence. Then, when they are feeling somewhat comfortable in the classroom, they can tackle the heavier philosophical issues. There are certainly arguments to be made for this approach, and faculties of education have debated its merits for decades. Obviously, there is no one best answer, or every program would teach the same topics in the same order. Although this text has been written with the intent of introducing foundational material first (because that is the way it is usually done), there is certainly no reason to avoid rearranging the order of the books.

Chapter 1 introduces an array of careers available to those who take coursework in early childhood education. It deals with such issues as remuneration (often not good), required training for different responsibilities, and good and bad reasons to choose careers in the field. Because early education is still in the midst of a longtime struggle for recognition as a true profession, chapter 1 also discusses this issue. There is a national need for teachers and caregivers who regard what they do with full respect—and expect others to do the same. Professional teaching standards as delineated by the foremost professional organizations are discussed in full. The chapter ends with an invitation to the reader to begin thinking philosophically, and the primary theories of early education are introduced.

In chapter 2 we meet the most influential leaders in the history of early childhood education. Although they were all products of their own nationalities, cultures, and centuries, their influence is still felt today in many of our classrooms and centers. This chapter shows clearly that the opinions we sometimes take for granted as the best ones often have their roots in the thinking of someone who died decades, even centuries, ago. It is true, too, that conflicts between differing viewpoints are generally based on thinking that evolved many years ago. Readers who believe that the best learning is structured, well planned, and goal focused will be interested to read about John Locke, a 17th-century Englishman. Those who are more drawn to a hands-off approach, in which young children run free and unencumbered by teachers' demands, will find their philosophical forefather in the 18th-century Jean Jacques Rousseau. Some of the other important figures described in this chapter themselves will have been influenced by either Locke or Rousseau or, perhaps, both.

Applying theoretical perspectives in actual early education sites is the subject of chapter 3. Seven schools and centers are described in some detail, and their links to theory and philosophy are explained. The reader should begin to see that successful teaching requires a foundation of thought rather than a simplistic presentation of apparently appealing activities. Each school or center is different in some ways from all the others, but each one also is committed to excellent experiences for children and was chosen for this book because of its success.

The United States has always been a nation of immigrants (even the prenation "native" Americans came from someplace else). In recent decades, however, the mix of nationalities and cultures providing new residents and citizens has become increasingly complex. With this new complexity has come the need to redefine what it means to be an American. In addition, the last half of the 20th century put into focus the inequality of education that had separated Blacks and Whites for centuries. Schools were forcibly desegregated, but inequalities remained. The second half of the century also brought a nationwide discussion of the best way to educate children with various disabilities. Experience and observation led many to believe that including these children in regular classrooms was the most advantageous for everyone. Laws were enacted to ensure just such a result. With momentous societal changes such as these, issues relating to our diverse culture now provide one of the most important chapters in any foundational textbook. Chapter 4 discusses first the changing face of America, then provides opportunity for readers to reflect on what all the changes mean to them as teachers. Finally, several cultures found commonly in centers and schools today are described. For each one, suggestions for interacting with families are given. It is important for readers to realize—and we mention this in the chapter continually—that not everyone within a particular culture acts or thinks in traditional ways. However, it is hoped that these descriptions help beginning teachers to think about their client families' beliefs, values, and needs before interacting with them.

Armed with the information provided by chapters 1 through 4, you should be ready to debate some of today's most difficult issues. Several of these are described in chapter 5, with documented arguments on varying sides of each one. From the hard-to-face reality of this culture's violence, to the television that we love to hate, and even to your own teacher education program, you should find some arguments worth having. You might argue the issues with your family, your roommates, your classmates, and even (or especially) within yourself. In any case, spend some time thinking through the various viewpoints, and challenge yourself to see things the way others do; you might even find your own opinions altering a bit.

Throughout this book, you are invited to develop your own philosophy of early childhood education. We hope that the information and ideas it provides give you sufficient foundation to make some major progress toward doing so. Consider writing and keeping your statement of philosophy, and plan to look back on it in a year and then again a few years after that. Doing so can be an important step away from stagnation and toward your continual growth as a teacher.

EARLY CHILDHOOD EDUCATION

YESTERDAY, TODAY, AND TOMORROW

1

CONTEMPORARY PERSPECTIVES: CAREERS, CONTEXTS, AND PRINCIPLES

America's future will be determined by the home and the school. The child becomes largely what it is taught, hence we must watch what we teach it, and how we live before it.

Jane Addams (1860–1935)

▼ *Chapter Objectives*

After reading this chapter, you should be able to:

▼ Explain the careers available to early childhood professionals and describe the settings in which they take place.

▼ Identify the major early childhood professional organizations.

▼ Describe the differences between appropriate and inappropriate reasons for choosing an early childhood career.

▼ List and explain the professional teaching standards of the early childhood professional.

▼ Describe the major philosophical traditions of early education.

As you think about and apply chapter content on your own, you should be able to:

▼ Begin to identify the best options for your own future career.

▼ Start formulating your own philosophy of early education.

Y ou have chosen to study early education at a time when the field is undergoing a period of growth and change. In the 1990s, research in early development became widely known among the general public as did the effects of early education on children characterized as at risk of failure in school. It was suddenly apparent that although love and kindness are vitally important for infants and young children, they are not sufficient for the kind of well-being that can take youngsters successfully into adulthood.

Brain research, for example, was beginning to explain the effects of very early experiences on humans' lifelong capacity to learn. Additionally, the long-term benefits of early education became apparent as a large group of low-income children of the 1960s—some urban, some rural—grew to adulthood, demonstrating greater successes in all aspects of life than did their unpreschooled counterparts.

Old, half-forgotten discussions were reopened nationwide, at all levels of society. The undervaluing of early educators as expressed in their insufficient pay was one new–old topic: Parking lot attendants and grocery clerks often made better wages. The high turnover of teachers and caregivers along with their lack of appropriate education was another topic, with due respect paid to the influence of low wages on the situation. Increasing numbers of state governments became interested in funding education for 3- and 4-year-olds, particularly for those at risk in their development or those from low-socioeconomic families.

Early childhood professionals were well prepared for this historic window of opportunity. Although late 20th-century findings from brain research were, in part, new, earlier studies and the development of theory had already alerted the profession to the importance of the early years. The discrepancy between the important task of fostering young children's development and the accompanying low levels of pay, of course, had been long and painfully obvious. Over the previous decade, there had been concerted efforts by early childhood professionals to deal with this issue. By the late 1990s, when a nationwide awareness of inadequate pay had evolved, position statements and the people to deliver them were ready and in place.

Taking leadership was the National Association for the Education of Young Children (NAEYC). Headquartered in Washington, DC, this organization had been growing in size and influence for many decades, until it had become the largest and best known organization devoted to the well being of young children. (As defined by NAEYC, *early childhood* comprises the years from birth to age 8.)

In the mid-1980s NAEYC, with support from other related organizations and many early educators and researchers, responded to developments in education that they found alarming. Although theory and research were making it increasingly apparent that young children learn best through active learning approaches, there was a widespread trend toward providing them with just the opposite: rote learning, out-of-context skills, too much whole-group instruction, and readiness tests that unfairly retained children or denied them enrollment entirely. NAEYC's response was to create a series of position papers that laid out the results of research, showing the inappropriateness of such trends in early education. These statements eventually led to a major document, published in 1987 and known as *Developmentally Appropriate Practice in Early Childhood Programs Serving Children from Birth through Age 8* (Bredecamp, 1987). Over the next decade, reactions from the field informed NAEYC of alterations that should be made to the document and of additional voices that needed to be heard as decisions about these modifications were made. The revised edition of the book was published in 1997 with accompanying video conferences for educational leaders. Thus, as public awareness of the importance of the early years arose, a nationwide network of early childhood professionals was ready to respond with shared knowledge and understanding of what was at stake.

Likewise, when the discussion of insufficient wages was reopened, the professionals were prepared. Over the same decade or more, there had been extensive discussion of what it meant to be a professional educator of young children and how levels of responsibility should be equitably and rationally divided. The result was another NAEYC document, *The Early Childhood Career Lattice: Perspectives on Professional Development* (Johnson & McCracken, 1994). We often think of professional growth in terms of a career *ladder*, but the concept of a career *lattice* was chosen to reflect the variety and complexity of the early childhood profession. The vertical strands of the lattice represent the many roles and settings available in the profession; these are crossed by horizontal levels ordinarily thought of as the career ladder that leads to increased responsibility and higher salary; finally, diagonals on the lattice demonstrate the movement that professionals can make across the various roles. Taken together, all these interconnected strands add up to the unique entity that is the early childhood profession.

The NAEYC creators of the career lattice concept noted two challenges that remained to be met, and some years later, these are still of concern. The first regards the historical but artificial separation of care and education for young children. In reality, youngsters learn continually from the world around them whether those in charge of them think they are offering education or not. On the other hand, people who designate themselves as teachers cannot foster growth in young children unless they include a strong element of care. Despite the fact that early care and education are intimately intertwined, they are generally funded and regulated by different agencies. It is also usually true that people officially engaged in caring are compensated less satisfactorily than people officially designated as teachers.

The second challenge affects special educators and those in general early education as well. Traditionally, children with special needs were separated from the larger population so that they could receive focused education and training. This is no longer always the case, with the concept of *inclusion* taking strong precedence over removal. This complicates the career lattice in all directions as teachers in general classrooms gain skills for working with special needs children, and vice versa, and as compensation for greater knowledge and skill is earned.

The trend toward inclusion of young children with special needs in early childhood programs is reflected in collaborative activities between NAEYC and the Division of Early Childhood (DEC). DEC is a national professional organization for early childhood special educators, a division of the Council of Exceptional Children (CEC). Membership in DEC has grown dramatically since the mid-1980s, when preschool special education became a national mandate in the United States. DEC provides leadership for the field of early childhood special education through publication of *The Journal of Early Intervention*, annual conferences, state chapters, training workshops, and position papers on current issues. The DEC and NAEYC alliance is a powerful force and resource on behalf of all young children and their families. Publications on inclusion can be found on each organization's Web site and in joint publications. (At the end of this, and all other chapters, you will find a list of pertinent Internet resources.)

There are a number of ways in which early childhood professionals can prepare themselves for their work. In general, the more years spent learning and the larger the number of credentials or certificates, the greater the remuneration and professional acceptance. Table 1.1 shows how this ordinarily works. It also demonstrates the complexity of the profession and the high level of preparation that is necessary if the education of young children is, at last, to be taken with full seriousness by our society.

The beginning of the 21st century, then, brings early childhood education to something of a crossroads. We can choose to move forward with providing experiences for children that reflect our rapidly expanding understanding of how they develop and learn. Or we can resist change—always uncomfortable, no matter how beneficial—and stay with more familiar but outdated methods of teaching. Additionally, we can gather our courage to demand the respect that should come from having prepared ourselves as professionals. Or we can simply complain about the unfairness of a cul-

TABLE 1.1

Early Childhood Positions, Credentials, and Responsibilities

Position	Minimum Education	Responsibilities
Director or principal	Usually BA or BS degree or MEd.	Oversees and manages enrollment, parent relations, curriculum, budget, general running of school.
Program or educational director, curriculum coordinator, resource teacher	Usually BA or BS or MEd, teaching experience.	Monitors programs, materials, and testing; coordinates curriculum; provides in-service programs and program development.
Head teacher	AA degree and/or CDA certificate, or BA or BS degree.	Coordinates curriculum and schedules, calls and runs meetings, represents teachers, may be responsible for personnel issues and aide training.
Teacher	AA degree and/or CDA certificate in preschools. BA or BS in K–3 grades; state certificate in public schools.	Designs curriculum, plans schedule, has primary teaching responsibility for a single class.
Associate or assistant teacher	Usually AA degree and/or CDA certificate.	Supervises and/or teaches under direction of teacher.
Teacher aide or teacher assistant	Depends on site or local regulations.	Helps teacher as directed.

ture that pays lip service to the value of children and the need for equitable wages and then acts inadequately. It is your generation of early childhood professionals that will be most responsible for deciding the directions that will be taken as the new century begins. Perhaps you don't as yet know which way you will go, or even if this will be your next or final career choice. As you read this book, take your education courses, and work in the field, reflect on the issues that face the profession of early childhood education and then determine your place in it.

SHOULD I CHOOSE TEACHING YOUNG CHILDREN AS MY PROFESSION?

> *Young children are interesting and appealing, but they are also sensitive and vulnerable. How we care for them, what we do and say each day affects their happiness and well-being as they grow. (Hendrick, 1987, p. 1)*

Young children soak up knowledge about their world with the eagerness of thirsty sponges. Because they don't yet have the cognitive sophistication to sort through those things that are valuable to learn and those that are less worthy, they take in just about everything. Thus, this quote by Joanne Hendrick, a leading writer in the field, suggests that people who work with young children have an ethical obligation to choose a career in early childhood education with serious intent and for the right reasons. Here are a few of those reasons, as suggested by Hendrick, with some observations to accompany them.

• *Because you like to teach.* It is possible, even probable, that you have had experiences with children already and that these have been sufficiently positive to lead you into the field. If you have not, then do acquire some experience before you go much further. After all, you probably wouldn't buy a car or even a suit without trying them out first. It is even more important to try out a career to be sure it fits you. If, on the other hand, you have had some experience but it has been of only one type, find time to try out some related options. Teaching Sunday school is quite different from spending an entire day with toddlers, which is quite different from teaching a classroom of second graders, and so on.

• *Because you can make an important difference in children's lives.* At the start of this chapter, we described briefly the long-term benefits of early preschool experiences for children born in poverty; those who attend preschool are found to reach adulthood with much more success in their professional and personal lives than those who do not. The research that has reported these benefits infers that what teachers of young children do has enormous impact! Because the growth in young children is often concrete and visible, one satisfaction for their teachers is seeing positive changes on a day-to-day basis. Perhaps a new kindergartner overcomes his shyness and asks to join others in the dramatic play area, and they accept him graciously. Or a whole class of 3-year-olds suddenly understands the art of getting both arms into their coat sleeves. Or a third grader who has been unable to relate rote-learned arithmetic tables to real life begins to show her understanding of the processes by creating story problems of her own. Such small victories collect and build to successful lives for children and satisfying careers for their teachers.

• *Because you can enrich the lives of the families you serve.* Children are tied to their families more intimately in the early years than at any other time in their lives. The ensuing three-way relationship among parents, teacher, and young child also tends to be closer than in later years. Parents are often welcomed into the classroom not just for formal and informal meetings but as observers or helpers too. Some careers in early childhood send the professional to the homes of the youngsters. Whatever the setting, the opportunities are many for communication about a child's growth and the effectiveness of various approaches to fostering that growth.

• *Because you like diversity and challenge.* People who teach young children are seldom able to rest on their past experiences but, rather, must prepare each day carefully, thinking through a variety of options before creating an hours-long schedule. Furthermore, that schedule generally includes long periods of time when several activities are occurring at once, and the teacher must be aware of what is happening with each activity at any given time. A kindergarten teacher once found herself dealing with the following: several boys in the block corner negotiating for increased space in the next-door housekeeping corner that was inhabited by three territorial and angry girls; one boy "flying" around the room knocking games and books off shelves; two children at a woodworking table having trouble sawing a piece of lumber; several others quietly looking at books in the library corner; three or four at the sand and water table that was just beginning to leak out one side; and all while she tried to get a stuck zipper opened for a boy who was in desperate need of the toilet. She could only laugh, realizing—as any teacher of young children must—that flexibility and a sense of humor are important traits for success in the early education profession.

• *Because you are needed.* The population of young children is growing and will continue to do so. As we continue to have high numbers of marriages with two parents working and single parents in need of child care while they work, the demand will be steady or will increase. As society and the workplace become more complex, making learning experiences from the earliest years of ever-greater importance, the need for caring, dedicated, well-educated professionals grows. Perhaps you should be one of them!

Although these reasons for choosing a career in early childhood are sound, there are others that, as Hendrick (1987) says, are "based on illusion rather than reality" (p. 5). She lists three that can be observed or heard frequently. If any of these is your primary reason for choosing this career direction, it might be a good time to reflect on your choice, perhaps spending more time in a teaching situation before making your final decision.

• *Because young children are so cute and lovable.* This reason is often stated as, "I just want to be a teacher because I love children and I always have." Of course it is good to love children, but as a primary reason to choose the profession, it comes up lacking. Almost no child is lovable at all times. Furthermore, in every group of

As the demand for child care increases, the need for caring professionals grows.

children there will be some who are easier to love than others. Frequently, it is the children who appear least lovable to adults who are most in need of adult attention and who may make the greatest strides in school, given proper care, teaching, and intervention. The professional teacher regards his or her children as real human beings and understands that they can be moody or calm, enthusiastic or disinterested, happily obedient or strongly independent. And sometimes cute.

• *Because young children are easier to control than older children.* Some prospective teachers have tried working with older children and have found management and discipline to be a barrier to success. They assume that working with younger, smaller children will be easier. This is definitely not the case! Young children are egocentric, as yet unable to see things very well from another's point of view. They haven't yet developed much skill at patience and want their way n-o-w. Although they will bend to the will of an authority figure while he or she is in view, they often revert to their own desires once the authority isn't looking. Furthermore, they are in constant motion, but tire quickly, and are impulsive rather than planful in their actions. It takes a skilled professional to know how to attain an atmosphere of well-managed calm in a classroom of younger children.

• *Working with young children is just baby sitting and play.* Yes, play happens in an effectively taught class. But it is assuredly not baby sitting, although caring for and about youngsters is always a crucial element of this work. Teachers of young children do not just provide play and hope or trust that learning will follow. For play to be an effective mode of learning, it must be carefully orchestrated, planned, and integrated with a wide variety of learning experiences. Successful teaching through play is a skill acquired through study and practice.

A career in early childhood education can be highly rewarding in many ways, particularly if it is chosen for some of the better reasons discussed previously. For the benefit of children as well as the career satisfaction of the teacher, it is also a career that should be chosen only by those who plan to take it seriously, as professionals.

WHAT IS A PROFESSIONAL?

The dictionary defines a *profession* as an occupation or vocation that requires advanced education and training as well as intellectual skills, and teaching is often included as an example. To be a *professional*, dictionaries tell us, requires an active commitment to the chosen profession's high standards.

One educator, researcher, and writer (Fromberg, 1997) lists six characteristics of a profession that expand on this definition:

• An expectation of ethical performance.
• The required high level of expertise and skill.
• A body of knowledge and skills not possessed by lay people.
• Considerable autonomy in its practice, including control of entry into the profession.
• Commensurate compensation.
• A professional organization.

To be a professional, then, requires a good amount of self-motivation, effort, and integrity. It also includes the need to continue one's education over a long period— probably for the duration of one's professional life—and to participate in, as well as agree to the tenets of, the applicable professional organizations.

More specifically, to be an early childhood professional, your task will be to fulfill your state's requirements for certification; demonstrate your capabilities as you interact with children; subscribe to the codes of ethics laid out by NAEYC and DEC; keep up-to-date on research, theory, and developments in the understanding of best practices; and participate at some level in your choice of professional organizations. To get you started along this road, we have included a copy of NAEYC's code of ethics in Appendix A; Appendix B is the code of ethics from DEC. At the end of this chapter, you will find a list of professional organizations that it will be helpful for you to know about. Think about the boxed statement you find here. It accompanies the NAEYC code of ethics and speaks to the commitment we need to make as early childhood professionals. Take a moment to reflect on your own readiness to adopt it.

STATEMENT OF COMMITMENT

As an individual who works with young children, I commit myself to furthering the values of early childhood education as they are reflected in the NAEYC Code of Ethical Conduct.

To the best of my ability I will

- Ensure that programs for young children are based on current knowledge of child development and early childhood education.
- Respect and support families in their task of nurturing children.
- Respect colleagues in early childhood education and support them in maintaining the NAEYC Code of Ethical Conduct.
- Serve as an advocate for children, their families, and their teachers in community and society.
- Maintain high standards of professional conduct.
- Recognize how personal values, opinions, and biases can affect professional judgment.
- Be open to new ideas and be willing to learn from the suggestions of others.
- Continue to learn, grow, and contribute as a professional.
- Honor the ideals and principles of the NAEYC Code of Ethical Conduct.

CAREER STANDARDS

In 1987, the National Board for Professional Teaching Standards (NBPTS) was founded by educators with support from school boards, college officials, business executives, and state governors. The core challenge embraced by the board was "delineating outstanding practice and recognizing those who achieve it" (National Association for the Education of Young Children [NAEYC], 1996, p. 55). The philosophical foundation underlying any definition of outstanding practice, the board proposed, should include five assumptions:

1. teachers are committed to students and their learning, treating them equitably while recognizing their individual differences;
2. teachers know the subjects they teach and how to teach them;
3. teachers are responsible for managing and monitoring student learning, and know how to engage students in disciplined learning;
4. teachers think systematically about their practice and learn from experience, exemplifying themselves the virtues they hope to instill in their students; and
5. teachers are members of learning communities, working with colleagues and parents to make decisions for their students' benefit.

While much of early education involves play, this is an insufficient reason
to choose teaching young children as a career.

From these five assumptions or propositions, age-related professional teaching
standards were developed. For the early childhood years, there are eight standards. It
is understood that these are standards to which only accomplished, experienced
teachers should be held. Think of them as goals for your not-too-distant future. They
are presented here in brief summary form; actual descriptions as available from the
NBTPS or NAEYC appear in much richer detail.

• *Understanding young children.* There are three ways in which teachers need to
understand their children: They must have a knowledge of universal principles of
physical, social and emotional, and cognitive development; they need informed
awareness of the roles that culture, history, and the values of community and family
have in children's development and learning; and they must know the attributes of the
children in their own classrooms. With a good understanding in all three areas, teachers are then able to plan programs to engage children in meaningful learning and to
assess their progress.

• *Promoting child development and learning.* Based on their understanding of
young children, teachers are able to structure a physical and social and emotional
environment that successfully fosters development and learning. Teachers are aware
of the importance of play in all aspects of children's development. They incorporate
play throughout the day and can explain its use as a learning tool to parents, colleagues, and administrators. To promote health and physical growth, teachers provide
both movement and rest, fine- and gross-motor activities, and education in health and

hygiene. To enhance social development, teachers educate children about behavioral expectations, learning in groups, and the importance and meaning of rules. To support emotional development and self-respect, teachers encourage independence, risk taking, and persistence. To foster language acquisition, teachers provide plenty of opportunities to use both oral and written language. And to encourage growth in knowledge, teachers provide appropriate resources and opportunities for children to engage their curiosity while learning to take risks, be persistent, and work with peers.

• *Knowledge of integrated curriculum.* Integrating the curriculum involves crossing academic disciplines to create learning that is personally relevant and meaningful to children. The core academic subjects for young children include literacy, language arts, mathematics, science, social studies, and the visual and performing arts. A multidisciplinary approach to teaching might include organizing a learning project according to key concepts, themes, or topics of interest to the children; in each case, appropriate learning would be pulled from each of the academic areas. Accomplished teachers have learned to do this to such an extent that the casual observer might find it difficult to sort out what subjects are being taught when. Still, teachers also know that each academic area has its own integrity, major ideas, and concepts and are sure to incorporate these within the learning experiences of their classes.

• *Multiple teaching strategies for meaningful learning.* Referring back to the first standard, we see that teachers need to be aware of universal development principles, cultural and societal influences, and the needs and interests of their individual children. The complexity of this awareness ultimately leads to complexity in teaching approaches. There is a good mix in the classroom of varying activities, discussions, and social interactions. Teachers must observe, listen, ask skilled questions, facilitate discussions, select and adapt materials, and know when to intervene and when to let children alone. They can arrange and rearrange the physical environment, including technology, to implement activities appropriately. Accomplished teachers recognize when children are developing outside the typical range or are learning English as a new language. They make curricular and environmental alterations as necessary, knowing when to seek assistance from others, including the families of these children.

• *Assessment.* Teachers need to judge the effects of their work and make decisions about the things that happen next in the classroom. They are also accountable to children and their parents as well as to the general public. Teachers of young children know that assessment of their work must go on daily as they observe youngsters working and playing, interacting socially, engaging themselves physically, and gaining cognitive knowledge. Their assessment strategies are varied and include observations, questions, listening, anecdotal records, systematic sampling of work products, and standardized instruments when they are appropriate.

• *Reflective practice.* Effective teachers engage in ongoing self-examination. They consider the role of their experiences, cultures, biases, and values on their decision making and interactions with children. They are open to innovation and positive change while being aware of the difference between important breakthroughs and momentary fads. They see the need for self-renewal to strengthen the quality of their

Effective teachers reflect continually on their work and seek to strengthen its quality through lifelong learning.

work and know that this means lifelong learning. As effective teachers reflect, they make use of and select from research studies, theories old and new, and current discussions about best practices. They continually look for ways to grow personally and professionally.

• *Family partnerships.* Accomplished teachers know that positive outcomes result from viewing families as allies in their work. They know that young children are especially dependent on their families and that children who feel as though home and school are well connected will be happier, more self-confident, and more motivated. These teachers know that families come in varying types and sizes and are respectful of them all. They are able to evaluate each parent's special abilities and interests and then engage them effectively in the classroom, with projects that can be done at home, or in support of their own children's growth. Important teacher skills include the ability to listen to and learn from family members as well as to share information about children's progress and events in the classroom. And they are able to share information about child development, as well as an understanding of child behavior, in ways that are useful to parents.

• *Professional partnerships.* This final standard is based on the need for teachers to take what they have demonstrated within the other standards and share their knowledge with others, to receive information from other knowledgeable professionals, and to work effectively with colleagues from all levels. Effective teachers can be supportive as they offer criticism and stay positive and open-minded as they receive it. They can skillfully challenge those who engage in behaviors that are detrimental to children, and they are diligent in finding other teachers' classroom activities to celebrate publicly. They give and attend workshops, network with others in the profession, participate in professional organizations, perhaps become involved in child-related community issues or service, and even write or make presentations about what they have learned and experienced as teachers.

The NBPTS early childhood committee responsible for delineating the eight standards just summarized, recognized that their expectations might "seem extraordinarily demanding," yet "every day they are upheld by teachers . . . who are hard at work in our schools inspiring the nation's children." The committee hoped that the standards would "promise to be a stimulus for self-reflection on the part of teachers at all levels of performance" (NAEYC, 1996, p. 101). Thus, they have been included here for you to think about as you consider the demands of a profession that has always been of critical importance but is only now beginning to be widely understood in that light.

CAREER CHOICES

An early childhood career provides a choice of age groups with which you can work. Although the early childhood years typically cover from birth to age 8, different programs divide these ages in different ways. Some schools and centers segregate each age group, making it possible to focus on the changing needs of the child at each identifiable stage. Others place two or more age groups together so that children can learn from each other and also share their growing knowledge and expertise. There are advantages and disadvantages to each approach, and as you work with children of different ages, you will no doubt discover that you have some preferences. There may even be some ages you are not comfortable working with at all. Try to identify your preferences and capabilities during your teacher education, as this is the time when it is easiest to experiment, take risks, and learn from others' feedback.

In addition to selecting particular age groups to work with, focus on specific roles within the early childhood profession. In part this will be determined by the level of training you undergo, but there is still quite a bit of flexibility. You may decide to own your own school, and that could mean caring for a small group of children in your home or creating a larger enterprise with its own buildings and a large staff. Eventually you might not work with children at all, preferring instead to become director of a center or even to attend law school and specialize in education-related legal issues. As a teacher, you can work with privately run centers that are either nonprofit or profit driven; teach in public preschools, kindergartens, or primary grades; or be employed in corporate care centers. Some public libraries hire people with early childhood training for their children's rooms, and there are hospitals that run nurseries for their patients or even the patients' visiting siblings. Wherever young children gather, there is a career waiting for you. Here are some of the more traditional jobs in early education, along with expected preparation, responsibilities, and rewards.

Teacher Aide or Teacher Assistant

This job requires little or no training, and the pay, which is minimum wage or close to it, reflects this. An aide helps the teacher in whatever ways are needed, usually assisting children in activities that require adult help: preparing supplies, grading projects and papers, keeping the environment cleaned and straightened. Primary qualifications for an aide are to enjoy, respect, and relate well to young children. Often, people who begin working with children by being an aide discover that they enjoy the work and would like to take more responsibility. Naturally, this requires more education. There may be people in your class now who have followed this route.

Associate Teacher or Assistant Teacher

An associate teacher has more credentials than a teacher aide, the most common being an associate of arts (AA) degree or a child development associate (CDA) certificate. The CDA program is offered by many community colleges and vocational–technical institutes that have early childhood programs, although it is also possible to be informally educated through in-service workshops. These programs require the student to demonstrate specific competencies in order to receive the certificate. The associate teacher, like the teacher aide, works under the direction of the regular teacher, usually in a center-based (as opposed to school-based) environment. The associate teacher supervises children as the teacher directs and may do some team teaching, particularly by reading stories or singing songs. Although this job generally pays more than the teacher aide position, the salary is still low.

Teacher, Including Regular and Special Education Preschool Teacher, and K–3 Entry-Level Teacher

In an early childhood center, a teacher will usually have an AA degree, possibly with the CDA certificate. Centers may also have teachers who hold bachelor's degrees, but the pay is generally lower than in the public schools, so this is less common. In public schools, kindergarten through the grades, entry-level teachers must have baccalaureate degrees, although some states are moving toward a required master's degree. As each state passes legislation to create publicly funded preschool education, decisions must be made concerning teacher training. In some cases, only an AA is required, thus lowering the personnel cost for the state; in others, a bachelor's degree is required.

In a school setting, the teacher is usually the highest level person to come in contact with the children. In early childhood centers, the teacher may also answer to a head teacher. In either case, the teacher makes lesson plans based on the school's philosophy and goals, arranges and maintains the environment, keeps records of children's progress, and does the actual day-to-day instructing.

Head Teacher

Typically found in an early childhood center or in special education public school preschool classrooms, the head teacher coordinates the curriculum and classroom functioning with the other teachers and staff. The head teacher takes a leadership role in meetings and planning sessions and may do some training of aides. Depending on the center and the head teacher's experience and capabilities, his or her background might include an AA, a bachelor's degree, or even a master's degree. Head teachers can often, but not always, expect to earn as much as public school teachers.

In public schools there may also be a head teacher, who is appointed by the principal or elected by other teachers, usually in the same grade. In this case, the head teacher is not expected to monitor the teaching or organization in other classrooms but coordinates the curriculum, calls meetings for the group, and speaks for the group in communications with administrators. There may well be no extra remuneration for this task, but the teaching load might be reduced in some way. Most people reading this book will be training to be a teacher or head teacher.

Program Director or Supervisor, Assistant Director, Educational Director, Curriculum Coordinator, or Resource Teacher

People in these positions have had experience, often in-depth, teaching young children. They have been successful at it and are willing to accept responsibility on a broader level. Their positions can be defined as a midway point between the administration and the teaching staff and generally provide pay that is above a teacher's but lower than an administrator's. These supervisors and coordinators are responsible for monitoring the programs of each teacher, coordinating curriculum, providing in-service programs, maintaining teaching materials, supervising testing, and spearheading program development. People in these positions may have an AA but can usually be expected to have at least a bachelor's degree and often some graduate work.

Director or Principal

Whatever the school setting, these positions require the most responsibility and the most unpredictable working hours. They also provide the highest pay. A director or principal must be able to work well with faculty, staff, parents, and the community as needed. In addition to overseeing the staff, this person must also manage the school's budget, coordinating it with the school's academic and caregiving goals. A director or principal generally holds a bachelor's degree and, increasingly, a master's or specialist's degree. In some places, principals and directors even hold doctoral degrees. In this case, they are usually expected to contribute professional research or extra programs for the community. Directors and principals have almost always had several years of teaching experience.

It is important to remember that parents and other family members are a child's first teachers, both chronologically and in importance.

As you take your courses and have opportunities to work in classrooms, centers, and homes, think about the settings within which you will feel most comfortable. Then, choose an appropriate career direction and try setting goals for the next 5 years or so. Finally, be sure that you are acquiring the necessary training and credentials when you need them. This advice might sound painfully obvious, but many prospective teachers ignore such suggestions and eventually find themselves taking redundant courses, going back to school for requirements they overlooked, or changing careers because the credentials they need require too much time, effort, and money. It is well worth the effort to think through now what professional roles you will want to play over the next several years. In looking forward to your future career, you will also want to consider the different settings available to you. The next section describes the most common ones.

WHERE YOUNG CHILDREN LEARN

This book is intended to provide the reader with information about being a teacher of young children, thus the focus of our discussion is on learning sites that have been created by adults. Yet it should always be remembered that humans begin to learn before birth and continue to do so for a considerable time before they enter an educational setting. Furthermore, even after adult-directed education begins, youngsters continue to learn both before and after school or caregiving hours. Parents and other family members are a child's first teachers, both chronologically and in importance. Professionals must always remember this and give these teachers the greatest respect, turning to them for advice and suggestions and with a willingness to collaborate in their child's education. Following are descriptions of other places young children learn.

Nursery School and Preschool

The concept of nurturing very young children lay behind the creation and naming of the *nursery school*. At the turn of this century, Margaret and Rachel McMillan noted with dismay the sad state of health of many of England's youngsters. The sisters were inspired to create a school designed to give children plenty of fresh air, good food, and hygiene in addition to academics and socialization through play. Their employees were qualified both as nurses and as teachers. When transported to the United States, nursery schools often became cooperatives, with parents sharing the responsibilities of running them, thus keeping costs down. Children who attend nursery schools are generally between the ages of 2 and 4, or even 5.

The term *preschool* is often used interchangeably with nursery school. It is, however, a more modern term, implying a strong focus on academics and socialization and less on nutrition and hygiene. Attendance ages are the same.

Early Intervention Services

Specialized services for infants and toddlers who experience disabilities or have delayed development have been available in the United States and Canada for more than 20 years. Early intervention services provide individually designed assessment, therapeutic, and developmental programs and are funded by a tenuous combination of federal, state and provincial, school district, and private sources. Current best practice guidelines (DEC, 1993) indicate that services for newborns to 3-year-olds be centered in the lives of individual families, with caregiving activities and parent–child relationships the primary context and content for intervention.

Early intervention professionals work across a variety of settings and with a number of professionals from other disciplines. They make visits to homes, hospitals, and center-based classrooms to assess, design, implement, and monitor developmental interventions in movement, socialization, cognition, self-care, and communication domains. They coordinate educational and developmental services with physical, occupational, and speech therapists; pediatricians; family-service specialists; and early childhood professionals. Because so much of early intervention work occurs within family and community settings, infant and toddler specialists must also be competent at working across cultures and with adults as well as with infants and toddlers.

Kindergarten

Typically, kindergarten is 1-year learning experience, immediately preceding first grade. As originally created in mid-19th-century Germany, it was for children between the ages of 4 and 6. In many countries it remains so today. The idea, as conceived by Friedrich Froebel (whom you will learn more about in chapter 2) was that kindergarten would be a bridge between home and the primary grades. As public schools in the United States added a 1-year kindergarten to their regular programs and as more and more children began to attend preschool and child care, the role of kindergarten began to change. It may still be a bridge between home and the primary grades for many children, but it has also become a transition experience following preschool or child care. Kindergarten curricula vary depending on the philosophy of the school or district. Traditionally, the focus was on play with one academic purpose—readiness for first grade. In recent years, kindergartens have become much more academic, a move that has produced some degree of controversy. You will become acquainted with the issues in coming chapters.

Transitional Kindergarten, Pre-First Grade, and Interim First Grade

Some children do not seem ready to enter the primary grades after 1 year of kindergarten. To ensure success in later years, transitional programs were created. Some educators believe that if children appear to be at risk for academic failure, it is better to hold them back at this time than later, when the feeling of failure can be more damaging, academic momentum is lost, friends may be forever separated. Others argue that the primary reasons for holding children back in kindergarten tend to indicate a first-grade education that is developmentally inappropriate for the age: Children do not yet understand letter–sound relationships, follow directions well, work easily on paper-and-pencil tasks, raise their hands to talk, or speak only in turn. Many states have some form of transitional kindergarten, and this may be a career option.

Developmental Preschool and Kindergarten

In the United States, federal legislation (Individuals with Disabilities Education Act, 1997) requires that local school districts provide special education services for all eligible children beginning at age 3. Half-day developmental preschool classrooms are the most common setting for delivery of specialized instruction and related therapeutic services for 3- to 6-year-olds. Because public schools do not routinely serve the general population of preschoolers, developmental preschools have traditionally served only children with disabilities and developmental delays. The benefits of inclusion, however, have prompted many districts to explore creative alternatives to self-contained special education classrooms for preschoolers. Many districts have begun to enroll typically developing preschool peers in developmental preschool classrooms, or to provide special education services to eligible children in community child-care and preschool programs.

The timing of kindergarten entry can be a complicated issue for young children with special needs. Youngsters who are eligible for special education services may have already attended public school programs for 2 or 3 years already by the time they are 5, yet many 5-year-olds with disabilities or delays lack the social and pre-academic skills expected in kindergarten. In addition to the transitional programs previously described, a number of larger American school districts have designed alternate models rather than adhering strictly to age 5 or a specific group of skills as kindergarten entry requirements. One such program is supplementary kindergarten, which young students attend every day and for increasingly longer days to receive additional instruction in preparation for first grade. Another model is the continuation of developmental services in a special education kindergarten classroom, sometimes offered as a supplementary program to regular kindergarten attendance.

The role of developmental preschool and kindergarten teachers emphasizes enhancement of specific skills that will increase children's chances of success in the primary grades. Families are still a big part of youngsters' lives during the preschool years, so teachers and parents work together as partners. Developmental services often include speech and motor therapies integrated into classroom activities and coordinated with the teacher's curriculum.

Head Start

Head Start is a federally funded preschool program for economically disadvantaged children. It primarily serves children over the age of 3, but there are some home-based services for younger ages, an Early Head Start for birth to age 3, and a few primary grade pilot programs. Although it is now comprehensive in scope, with benefits for the entire family, Head Start was begun in 1965 as a summer-only program focusing on prekindergartners' health and social development. President Lyndon Johnson's War on Poverty promoted much creative thinking from the various governmental "warriors," and a number of social programs were begun almost simultaneously. Head Start was one of them and was viewed as a way to close the gap between the lives of economically disadvantaged children and those of their wealthier peers during the summer before the start of school. Today, children may attend Head Start for 2 years, and programs have academic orientations along with health and socialization. Chapter 3 describes several current Head Start programs in depth.

Primary Grades

Traditionally, early childhood education has been thought of as encompassing children from birth to age 8. In some ways, ages 6 to 8 are transitional years between early and middle childhood. The primary grades, 1 through 3, are concerned with educating children during this transition. The changes that begin to occur in youngsters' lives cover all aspects of their development. Socially, they become less focused on self and more interested in group interactions, less concerned with what adults think of them than with the opinions of their peers. Physically, they become more stable; more able to accomplish the fundamental movements that will enable them to participate in sports; and more adept at hand–eye coordination, leading to the ability to do pencil-and-paper or computerized school work. Cognitively, they begin to understand the world as adults see it, making academic learning possible.

Of course, not every child attains the same understandings and skills at exactly the same time in just the same way. Because children develop so unevenly during these years, it is important that primary teachers have a strong understanding of child development. Thus you will observe that teachers in the first three grades often have training in early childhood as well as in elementary education. Primary teachers are charged with introducing young children to all the academic subjects they will encounter for the next several years of their lives: literacy, oral and written language, mathematics, science, social studies, and the arts. However, because these are transitional years, separating the subject areas and teaching them formally is not usually the best approach. Primary-grade teachers generally find themselves seeking ways to integrate the curriculum into more meaningful themes, topics, or projects.

Child Care

The purpose of child care is to provide a secure and happy place for young children while their parents work. Typically it serves children from birth to school age, but it can also provide after-school care for older children. Types of child-care centers vary widely. Family day care is common and popular and is usually provided by a mother who wishes to stay home with her own children while earning income by caring for other children as well. Corporate or employer child care is provided by a company for its employees, although outsiders are often permitted if space is available. (Chapter 3 describes a corporate model in depth.) Proprietary child care is offered by for-profit organizations, some of them regional or national chains or franchises. Educational components in child-care settings vary widely and at times may not exist at all.

In many countries, child care is supported for all working parents by public money, but this has not been the case in the United States. Finding good care continues to be a nationwide problem for many families. It is an especially difficult problem for poor single parents in states with welfare-to-work laws. Just as their work skills increase sufficiently to apply for entry-level jobs and their welfare payments run out, they are faced with an inability to find affordable child care. In recent years, some states have developed child-care networks and referral agencies that provide parents with information on licensed centers and financial assistance.

GUIDING PHILOSOPHIES

Beyond choosing your career role and venue, there is another decision to be made, equally as important. Any kind of teacher in any setting must be able to knowledgeably choose materials for learning, activities to fill the day, management and discipline options, and teacher–child interaction styles. Learning how to make these decisions comprises much of a college student's teacher education program. Underlying this learning must be the development of a philosophy of early education.

From the time of the ancient Greeks until today, such philosophies have emerged, been tried, disappeared, and occasionally reappeared. At the beginning of the 21st century, there is no single philosophical orientation that is subscribed to by every educator of young children, but there are general categories that can be described.

Three Orientations to Early Education

A major component in successful teaching is a teacher's awareness of the students' intellectual, social, and emotional maturity. This is true whether the students are teenagers taking driver's training, middle schoolers meeting their first algebra class, or 3-year-olds learning a new singing game. However, in the case of children in the early years, the teacher's awareness of development is most important because young children change so rapidly. Their developmental status and their learning capacity are more intertwined than at any other time in their lives.

For this reason, research and philosophy related to early education have been dominated by psychological theorists as well as educators. In this section we look at three orientations to education: behaviorist, maturationist, and constructivist. All three are based in psychology, and the second and third are grounded in theories of development. Each orientation is intimately associated with the people who created it, and they are introduced in each section. Because these theorists have been so influential to early education, they are also described more fully in chapter 2.

The Behaviorist Orientation

At the beginning of the 20th century, psychology (along with many other fields) was moving toward a more scientific orientation. Carefully controlled experiments on animals were used as inspiration for the study of humans, including very young children. These influences on this new way of observing children can be traced to the 17th-century English philosopher, John Locke[1] who regarded children's minds as blank slates, ready to be written on by the environment. Although Locke would agree that heredity plays some part in a child's makeup and capacity for learning, he believed that external forces determined most of a child's progress. External forces included teaching materials and techniques as well as an appropriate approach to discipline. The latter, he argued, should be positive when possible and should almost never include corporal punishment.

Locke's views are echoed by modern-day *behaviorism*, the scientific approach to psychology and education that emerged in the early 1900s. The person most associated with behaviorism, particularly in relation to classroom applications, has been B. F. Skinner. Skinner's two primary contributions to education were the teaching machines (now replaced by computers) that made programmed learning possible and behavior modification, which produced new approaches to motivation and discipline. The behaviorist orientation includes the following concepts.

Behavior.   There are two types of behavior: reflexive, such as a knee jerk or eye blink, and operant, or voluntary. Operant behaviors, which are the focus of education, are controlled by their consequences, that is, by the pleasure (positive consequences) or pain (negative consequences) they produce. Behaviorists believe that careful struc-

---

[1]Locke and other historical figures described in this section are identified, dated, and cited more fully in chapter 2.

turing of the environment can produce desired social and cognitive behavior patterns in children.

Positive Reinforcement.   The frequency of desired behaviors can be increased by giving special food, toys, praise, hugs, or anything else the child sees as positive. For example, extra time on the playground is a positive reinforcer for most children and can be used as a motivator for academic work.

Negative Reinforcement.   Instead of adding a rewarding consequence, as in positive reinforcement, something aversive is taken away. For example, a child who is being disruptive during circle time may be required to sit next to an adult, whose hand stays on his shoulder during the ensuing activities. When the adult perceives that the child has calmed down, the hand is removed, and the child is once again permitted to participate freely. (This only works, of course, if the child does not consider sitting next to the adult a special treat.)

Punishment.   Skinner objected to punishment because of its undesirable side effects: anger, dislike of school, and the return of the undesired behavior. Researchers have found that punishment can change behavior, but it must be administered soon after the undesired behavior takes place.

Nonreinforcement.   In this case, the teacher simply ignores a behavior, either good or bad. A reason to ignore good behavior might be that it is time to wean a child from an expectation of continual rewards. In the case of bad behavior, nonreinforcement can often cause a child to stop the behavior because there is no reward in it.

Behavior Modification.   A child's behavior is modified, or changed, through the use of any of the methods just listed.

Teachers who subscribe to the behaviorist orientation must have very clear goals, and these must be stated behaviorally. For example, it is not enough to say that your class will understand addition. A specific goal must be established, such as attaining a score of 90% on a 5-minute written quiz of addition problems with sums of 10 or below.

Learning is generally sequenced, moving from the simple to the more complex, from the concrete to the abstract. Usually, larger bodies of knowledge are broken down into more manageable pieces. The goals of learning are defined by the teacher, not the children, and the teacher controls the way in which reinforcements are used to help achieve success.

A number of program models have been created based on the behaviorist orientation, and most teachers occasionally use some aspects of behaviorist theory, even if only informally, but it is in special education that behaviorist techniques are most pervasive. The clear-cut, straightforward approach, with learning broken down into small chunks, has had much appeal for those who use specialized instructional strategies to teach specific academic and social skills.

The Maturationist Orientation

A second move in the early 20th century toward a more scientific view of child development led to the maturationist orientation. Its roots can be traced to another philosopher, Jean Jacques Rousseau, a Swiss whose 18th-century writings were partly responsible for the French Revolution. Rousseau saw children not as blank slates but as inherently good and needing only proper nurturing to achieve their full potential, just as any plant matures according to a predetermined plan as long as it is given reasonable nourishment. In practice a teacher must provide an environment conducive to a child's progress, but the focus on nurturing the child's preprogrammed development is greater than on manipulating the environment to create a successful human being.

In the 20th century, Arnold Gesell became the leader in updating Rousseau's thoughts for a scientific age. Basing his theory on observation of large numbers of young children, Gesell argued that much of a child's development takes place in invariant, predictable stages. Each stage is a major step forward, and after it is reached, there is a period of consolidation before the next major step is taken. Other principles of the maturationist orientation include those discussed next.

Norms.   Decades of observing children led Gesell to define what children are like and what they should be able to do at specific ages. These developmental expectations or norms were made for each 6-month period of life.

Readiness.   Children should not be pushed into kindergarten or first grade just because they have reached a certain chronological age. First, they should be tested to see if they have reached prescribed intellectual and physical norms. If not, they should be held back until they are ready. Similarly, children should not be forced to read until they have reached their own internal maturational level of at least 6 years.

Children in a maturationist classroom are all at about the same stage of development. The teacher and the classroom environment nurture children but don't push them. Materials and activities are chosen because they are appropriate for the developmental stage of the children in the class. If children avoid them, this is a signal to the teacher that the level may be inappropriate and not that some sort of reinforcement might make them more attractive. The teacher's role is "acceptance, gentle guidance, and facilitation of children's wants and interests," but "directing, correcting, or actively modifying behavior are questionable or undesirable" (Lay-Dopyera & Dopyera, 1990, p. 172).

The Constructivist Orientation

Constructivist theories of how children learn developed about the same time as behaviorist and maturationist theories, but they did not reach the United States until the middle of the 20th century. From Russia came the ideas of Lev Vygotsky, but not until they were no longer suppressed by the repressive Soviet government of Joseph Stalin and finally could be translated into English. From Switzerland came the theories of Jean Piaget, but his dense writing style was daunting to many readers, even when translated into English, and the selection of his own children as his research subjects was suspect, so it was several decades before he gained acceptance in this country.

Of the two theorists, Piaget became widely known first, and his views offered a contradictory perspective to both behaviorism and maturationism. Whereas Piaget agreed that the environment influences child development and that there is a biological sameness among humans, he also argued that children help construct their own intelligence through active exploration of their individual environments. To Piaget, a child's biology is the primary factor in learning that comes right after birth. But, as time goes by, the child has more input from the environment and from social experiences, and these factors become more important than biology. By the time the child enters preschool, the environment and social experiences are primary influences in learning. Yet, the child does not just passively absorb the environment but actively operates on it and, in the process, constructs his or her own intelligence.

As children learn, they progress through stages, but the constructivist's view of these stages is a bit different from the maturationist's. The maturationist sees stage development as a predetermined, natural, flowerlike unfoldment; the constructivist argues that this is only part of the picture. When children actively operate on the environment, their experiences influence their maturational processes. Thus, their learning is determined both by environmental influences and by maturation.

Piaget's ideas were taking hold among a vast number of early childhood thinkers, researchers, and educators when Vygotsky's work was translated into English in the early 1960s. Because of Piaget's popularity, it was another two decades before Vygotsky's views were accepted too. The two men's ideas were generally complementary, but their basic philosophies of how the world should work created some distance.

Piaget came from the long and strong democratic tradition of his country. His belief in the rights of the individual led to a theory of development that gives due respect to the powers of the individual child in self-construction. Vygotsky, on the other hand, graduated from Moscow University in the same year as the beginning of his country's communist revolution. Having been a cruelly repressed Jew in the czarist years, Vygotsky quickly grasped the idealism of the new socialist state. Quite naturally, he developed a theory that suggests the need for social interaction as a major element in a child's self-construction.

As translated into classroom practice, the two theories lead to slightly different approaches to teaching. (Piaget wrote about education with some reluctance since he was primarily interested in the development of knowledge. Vygotsky embraced the challenge and added pedagogy to his psychological studies.) In a more Piagetian classroom, children can be seen directing their own learning to the extent that their maturity permits them. In a more Vygotskian setting, adults and more knowledgeable peers will intervene more often and earlier in the learning process. The first method respects the child's individualistic approach to learning, whereas the second pays homage to the power of the group. You will undoubtedly find a place for both approaches in your own work.

In any situation, however, there are some notable differences between the constructivist classroom and the behaviorist or maturationist. The carefully sequenced small bits of knowledge favored by behaviorists give children little opportunity to carry out the kind of exploratory learning and play that constructivists feel is needed. The maturationists' use of developmental stages as a guide for planning is seen by constructivists as an insufficient framework for understanding early learning. In the latters' view, the goals of learning are not so much a predetermined set of facts or a particular level of accomplishment but opportunities for children to add onto their existing mental structures through active learning. They are likely to be found experimenting, questioning, and planning. Learning periods tend to be long and unstructured rather than neat and orderly.

Summary

These three orientations to learning are quite different from each other. Although you will find schools and centers that profess to be aligned with one or another of them, it is more likely that you will see a mixture of two or even all three at the same site. For example, you might visit a transitional kindergarten (maturationist) that teaches arithmetic through repeated drills (behaviorist) and has a long afternoon period when children experiment freely with many kinds of materials (constructivist).

EXTENDING YOUR LEARNING

1. From the career options discussed in this chapter, choose at least two that interest you. Interview someone who holds each position. Some questions you might ask:
   - What prompted you to choose this career?
   - What are your goals for the future? Will you continue with this indefinitely?
   - What are the most satisfying elements of your career? The most frustrating?
   - What are some ways I can prepare well for this kind of career?
   - What characteristics do you think someone needs to do this?

2. Observe a nursery school class and a primary grade class. List similarities and differences in the teacher's style, children's interactions with each other, children's interactions with the teacher, kinds of materials, and the amount of freedom the children have.

3. Observe a center or classroom for 30 minutes, writing down everything that happens. Then, make a map of the room(s), noting the principal materials and furnishings. Refer to the orientations toward early education described in this chapter, and determine which elements of each you observed. Try to identify the primary orientation of the site.

4. Write a beginning statement of your own philosophy of early childhood education. Save it for later reflection as you continue to learn more from your studies and practical experiences. At the end of each term, rewrite the philosophy as you see fit, but do keep the earlier versions so that you can see your own thinking emerge.

PROFESSIONAL ORGANIZATIONS

American Montessori Society
281 Park Ave. S., 6th Floor
New York, NY 10010–6102
212–358–1250

Association Montessori Internationale
AMI/USA
410 Alexander St.
Rochester, NY
716–461–5920
Bethesda, MD
716–461–5920

Association for Childhood Education International
17904 Georgia Ave., Suite 215
Olney, MD 20832
301–570–2111
800–423–3563

Center for the Child Care Workforce
733 15th St. NW
Washington, DC 2000–2112
202–737–7700

Council for Early Childhood Professional Recognition Child Development
Associate National Credentialing Program
1341 G St. NW, Suite 400
Washington, DC 20005
202–265–9090
800–424–4310

Council for Exceptional Children
1920 Association Dr.
Reston, VA 20191–1589
703–620–3660
800–CEC–SPED

Head Start Bureau
Administration for Children and Families
Department of Health and Human Services
P.O. Box 1182
Washington, DC 20013
800–377–4950

National Association for the Education of Young Children
1509 16th St. NW
Washington, DC 20036
202–232–8777
800–424–2460

National Black Child Institute
1023 15th St. NW, Suite 600
Washington, DC 20005
202–387–1281

INTERNET RESOURCES

Web sites provide much useful information for educators and we list some here that pertain to the topics covered in this chapter. The addresses of Web sites can also change, however, and new ones are continually added. Thus, this list should be considered as a first step in your acquisition of a larger and ever-changing collection.

American Montessori Society
  www.amshq.org

Association Montessori Internationale
  www.ami.edu

Center for the Child Care Workforce
  ericps.crc.uiuc.edu

Child Welfare League of America
  www.cwla.org

Children's Defense Fund
  www.childrensdefense.org

Division for Early Childhood, Council for Exceptional Children
  www.dec-sped.org

Head Start
  www.acf.dhhs.gov/programs/hsb

National Association for the Education of Young Children
  www.naeyc.org

Stand for Children
  www.stand.org

VOCABULARY

Behaviorism.   A term coined by the U.S. psychologist John Watson. The theory that observed behavior provides the only valid data of psychology.

Child Care Centers.   Facilities in which children are cared for. Centers may offer educational programs or simply custodial supervision.

Child Development Associate (CDA).   A graduate of a program offering the CDA certificate. CDA programs are usually offered in community colleges or vocational institutes and focus specifically on training for effective child care.

Constructivism.   A psychological theory largely attributed to the Swiss Jean Piaget. It postulates that humans construct their own knowledge, intelligence, and morality through a series of stages.

Kindergarten.   A German word meaning "children's garden" first coined by educator Friedrich Froebel in the mid-19th century. An educational setting for children about 5 years old.

Kindergartner.   Child of kindergarten age. A kindergarten teacher (obsolete).

Maturationism.   A psychological theory largely attributed to the U.S. psychologist Arnold Gesell. It holds that humans are biologically destined to mature in a regular, sequential pattern.

Negative Reinforcement.   Removal of something the subject does not like immediately following a halt in unwanted behavior and a return to appropriate behavior. Its purpose is to increase the likelihood that the positive behavior will occur more often in the future.

Nursery School.   A school for young children, typically between the ages of 2 and 5; a less academic preschool.

Positive Reinforcement.   Presentation of a reward, contingent on positive behavior. Its purpose is to increase the likelihood that the positive behavior will occur more often in the future.

Preschool.   A school for young children typically between the ages of 2 and 5; a more academic nursery school.

Transitional Kindergarten.   A class, midway between kindergarten and first grade, for children who are old enough to be in first grade but not considered ready for school learning.

References

Bredecamp, S. (Ed.). (1987). *Developmentally appropriate practice in early childhood programs serving children from birth through age 8.* Washington, DC: National Association for the Education of Young Children.

Bredecamp, S., & Copple, C. (Eds.). (1997). *Developmentally appropriate practice in early childhood programs (Rev. ed.).* Washington, DC: National Association for the Education of Young Children.

DEC Task Force on Recommended Practices. (1993). *DEC recommended practices: Indicators of quality in programs for infants and young children with special needs and their families.* Reston, VA: Division for Early Childhood, Council for Exceptional Children.

Hendrick, J. (1987). *Why teach? A first look at working with young children.* Washington, DC: National Association for the Education of Young Children.

Johnson, J., & McCracken, J. (Eds.). (1994). *The early childhood career lattice: Perspectives on professional development.* Washington, DC: National Association for the Education of Young Children.

Lay-Dopyera, M., & Dopyera, J. (1990). The child-centered curriculum. In Seefeldt, C. (Ed.), *Continuing issues in early childhood education.* Columbus, OH: Merrill.

Lay-Dopyera, M., & Dopyera, J. (1993). *Becoming a teacher of young children.* New York: McGraw-Hill.

National Association for the Education of Young Children. (1996). *Guidelines for preparation of early childhood professionals.* Washington, DC: Author.

APPENDIX A: NAEYC CODE OF ETHICAL CONDUCT AND STATEMENT OF COMMITMENT. GUIDELINES FOR RESPONSIBLE BEHAVIOR IN EARLY CHILDHOOD EDUCATION

This Code of Ethical Conduct and Statement of Commitment was prepared under the auspices of the Ethics Commission of the National Association for the Education of Young Children. Stephanie Feeney and Kenneth Kipnis did extensive research and prepared a "Draft Code of Ethics and Statement of Commitment." Following a five-year process involving the NAEYC membership, the Code of Ethical Conduct and Statement of Commitment was approved by NAEYC s Governing Board in July 1989.

Responsibility for reviewing the Code and preparing recommendations for revisions is assigned to NAEYC's Panel on Professional Ethics in Early Childhood Education. The first set of revisions was adopted in 1992 and the second set was approved by NAEYC's Governing Board in November 1997. The Code is reviewed for possible revision every five years.

The Statement of Commitment accompanying the Code is a recognition that the ultimate strength of the Code rests in the adherence of individual educators.

***

Stephanie Feeney, Ph.D., is Professor and Early Childhood Education Specialist at the University of Hawaii at Manoa. She is a former member of NAEYC's Governing Board.

Kenneth Kipnis, Ph.D., Professor of Philosophy at the University of Hawaii at Manoa, has written on legal philosophy and ethical issues in law, medicine, engineering, and other professions.

Financial assistance for developing the original Code was provided by NAEYC, the Wallace Alexander Gerbode Foundation, and the University of Hawaii.

An 11" × 14" companion poster for this brochure with the NAEYC Statement of Commitment is available from NAEYC for $2. **NAEYC order #450.**

Articles featuring an ethical dilemma or problem, and a variety of responses to it, often appear in *Young Children*, NAEYC's professional journal. These articles are designed for discussion by students and staff.

CODE OF ETHICAL CONDUCT

Preamble

NAEYC recognizes that many daily decisions required of those who work with young children are of a moral and ethical nature. The NAEYC Code of Ethical Conduct offers guidelines for responsible behavior and sets forth a common basis for resolving the principal ethical dilemmas encountered in early childhood care and education. The primary focus is on daily practice with children and their families in programs for children from birth through 8 years of age, such as infant/toddler programs, preschools, child care centers, family child care homes, kindergartens, and primary classrooms. Many of the provisions also apply to specialists, who do not work directly with children, including program administrators, parent and vocational educators, college professors, and child care licensing specialists.

Core values

Standards of ethical behavior in early childhood care and education are based on commitment to core values that are deeply rooted in the history of our field. We have committed ourselves to

- Appreciating childhood as a unique and valuable stage of the human life cycle
- Basing our work with children on knowledge of child development
- Appreciating and supporting the close ties between the child and family
- Recognizing that children are best understood and supported in the context of family, culture, community, and society
- Respecting the dignity, worth, and uniqueness of each individual (child, family member, and colleague)
- Helping children and adults achieve their full potential in the context of relationships that are based on trust, respect, and positive regard

Conceptual framework

The Code sets forth a conception of our professional responsibilities in four sections, each addressing an arena of professional relationships: (1) children, (2) families, (3) colleagues, and (4) community and society. Each section includes an introduction to the primary responsibilities of the early childhood practitioner in that arena, a set of ideals pointing in the direction of exemplary professional practice, and a set of principles defining practices that are required, prohibited, and permitted.

The ideals reflect the aspirations of practitioners. **The principles** are intended to guide conduct and assist practitioners in resolving ethical dilemmas encountered in the field. There is not necessarily a corresponding principle for each ideal. Both ideals and principles are intended to direct practitioners to those questions which, when responsibly answered, will provide the basis for conscientious decisionmaking. While the Code provides specific direction and suggestions for addressing some ethical dilemmas, many others will require the practitioner to combine the guidance of the Code with sound professional judgment.

The ideals and principles in this Code present a shared conception of professional responsibility that affirms our commitment to the core values of our field. The Code publicly acknowledges the responsibilities that we in the field have assumed and in so doing supports ethical behavior in our work. Practitioners who face ethical dilemmas are urged to seek guidance in the applicable parts of this Code and in the spirit that informs the whole.

Ethical dilemmas always exist

Often, "the right answer"—the best ethical course of action to take—is not obvious. There may be no readily apparent, positive way to handle a situation. One important value may contradict another. When we are caught "on the horns of a dilemma," it is our professional responsibility to consult with all relevant parties in seeking the most ethical course of action to take.

Section I: Ethical responsibilities to children

Childhood is a unique and valuable stage in the life cycle. Our paramount responsibility is to provide safe, healthy, nurturing, and responsive settings for children. We are committed to supporting children's development, respecting individual differences, helping children learn to live and work cooperatively, and promoting health, self-awareness, competence, self-worth, and resiliency.

Ideals:

I-1.1—To be familiar with the knowledge base of early childhood care and education and to keep current through continuing education and in-service training.

I-1.2—To base program practices upon current knowledge in the field of child development and related disciplines and upon particular knowledge of each child.

I-1.3—To recognize and respect the uniqueness and the potential of each child.

I-1.4—To appreciate the special vulnerability of children.

I-1.5—To create and maintain safe and healthy settings that foster children's social, emotional, intellectual, and physical development and that respect their dignity and their contributions.

I-1.6—To support the right of each child to play and learn in inclusive early child-hood programs to the fullest extent consistent with the best interests of all involved. As with adults who are disabled in the larger community, children with disabilities are ideally served in the same settings in which they would participate if they did not have a disability.

I-1.7—To ensure that children with disabilities have access to appropriate and con-venient support services and to advocate for the resources necessary to provide the most appropriate settings for all children.

Principles:

P-1.1—Above all, we shall not harm children. We shall not participate in prac-tices that are disrespectful, degrading, dangerous, exploitative, intimidating, emotionally damaging, or physically harmful to children. *This principle has precedence over all others in this Code.*

P-1.2—We shall not participate in practices that discriminate against children by denying benefits, giving special advantages, or excluding them from programs or activities on the basis of their race, ethnicity, religion, sex, national origin, lan-guage, ability, or the status, behavior, or beliefs of their parents. (This principle does not apply to programs that have a lawful mandate to provide services to a par-ticular population of children.)

P-1.3—We shall involve all of those with relevant knowledge (including staff and parents) in decisions concerning a child.

P-1.4—For every child we shall implement adaptations in teaching strategies, learning environment, and curricula, consult with the family, and seek recom-mendations from appropriate specialists to maximize the potential of the child to benefit from the program. If, after these efforts have been made to work with a child and family, the child does not appear to be benefiting from a program, or the child is seriously jeopardizing the ability of other children to benefit from the program, we shall communicate with the family and appropriate specialists to determine the child's current needs, identify the setting and services most suited to meeting these needs, and assist the family in placing the child in an appropriate setting.

P-1.5—We shall be familiar with the symptoms of child abuse, including physical, sexual, verbal, and emotional abuse, and neglect. We shall know and follow state laws and community procedures that protect children against abuse and neglect.

P-1.6—When we have reasonable cause to suspect child abuse or neglect, we shall report it to the appropriate community agency and follow up to ensure that appro-priate action has been taken. When appropriate, parents or guardians will be informed that the referral has been made.

P-1.7—When another person tells us of a suspicion that a child is being abused or neglected, we shall assist that person in taking appropriate action to protect the child.

P-1.8—When a child protective agency fails to provide adequate protection for abused or neglected children, we acknowledge a collective ethical responsibility to work toward improvement of these services.

P-1.9—When we become aware of a practice or situation that endangers the health or safety of children, but has not been previously known to do so, we have an ethical responsibility to inform those who can remedy the situation and who can protect children from similar danger.

Section II: Ethical responsibilities to families

Families are of primary importance in children's development. (The term *family* may include others, besides parents, who are responsibly involved with the child.) Because the family and the early childhood practitioner have a common interest in the child's welfare, we acknowledge a primary responsibility to bring about collaboration between the home and school in ways that enhance the child's development.

Ideals:

I-2.1—To develop relationships of mutual trust with families we serve.

I-2.2—To acknowledge and build upon strengths and competencies as we support families in their task of nurturing children.

I-2.3—To respect the dignity of each family and its culture, language, customs, and beliefs.

I-2.4—To respect families, childrearing values and their right to make decisions for their children.

I-2.5—To interpret each child's progress to parents within the framework of a developmental perspective and to help families understand and appreciate the value of developmentally appropriate early childhood practices.

I-2.6—To help family members improve their understanding of their children and to enhance their skills as parents.

I-2.7—To participate in building support networks for families by providing them with opportunities to interact with program staff, other families, community resources, and professional services.

Principles:

P-2.1—We shall not deny family members access to their child's classroom or program setting.

P-2.2—We shall inform families of program philosophy, policies, and personnel qualifications, and explain why we teach as we do—which should be in accordance with our ethical responsibilities to children (see Section I).

P-2.3—We shall inform families of and, when appropriate, involve them in policy decisions.

P-2.4—We shall involve families in significant decisions affecting their child.

P-2.5—We shall inform the family of accidents involving their child, of risks such as exposures to contagious disease that may result in infection, and of occurrences that might result in emotional stress.

P-2.6—To improve the quality of early childhood care and education, we shall cooperate with qualified child development researchers. Families shall be fully informed of any proposed research projects involving their children and shall have the opportunity to give or withhold consent without penalty. We shall not permit or participate in research that could in any way hinder the education, development, or well-being of children.

P-2.7—We shall not engage in or support exploitation of families. We shall not use our relationship with a family for private advantage or personal gain, or enter into relationships with family members that might impair our effectiveness in working with children.

P-2.8—We shall develop written policies for the protection of confidentiality and the disclosure of children's records. These policy documents shall be made available to all program personnel and families. Disclosure of children's records beyond family members, program personnel, and consultants having an obligation of confidentiality shall require familial consent (except in cases of abuse or neglect).

P-2.9—We shall maintain confidentiality and shall respect the family's right to privacy, refraining from disclosure of confidential information and intrusion into family life. However, when we have reason to believe that a child's welfare is at risk, it is permissible to share confidential information with agencies and individuals who may be able to intervene in the child's interest.

P-2.10—In cases when family members are in conflict, we shall work openly, sharing our observations of the child, to help all parties involved make informed decisions. We shall refrain from becoming an advocate for one party.

P-2.11—We shall be familiar with and appropriately use community resources and professional services that support families. After a referral has been made, we shall follow up to ensure that services have been appropriately provided.

Section III: Ethical responsibilities to colleagues

In a caring, cooperative workplace, human dignity is respected, professional satisfaction is promoted, and positive relationships are modeled. Based upon our core values, our primary responsibility in this arena is to establish and maintain settings and relationships that support productive work and meet professional needs. The same ideals that apply to children are inherent in our responsibilities to adults.

A—Responsibilities to co-workers

Ideals:

I-3A.1—To establish and maintain relationships of respect, trust, and cooperation with co-workers.

I-3A.2—To share resources and information with co-workers.

I-3A.3—To support co-workers in meeting their professional needs and in their professional development.

I-3A.4—To accord co-workers due recognition of professional achievement.

Principles:

P-3A.1—When we have a concern about the professional behavior of a co-worker, we shall first let that person know of our concern, in a way that shows respect for personal dignity and for the diversity to be found among staff members, and then attempt to resolve the matter collegially.

P-3A.2—We shall exercise care in expressing views regarding the personal attributes or professional conduct of co-workers. Statements should be based on firsthand knowledge and relevant to the interests of children and programs.

B—Responsibilities to employers

Ideals:

I-3B.1—To assist the program in providing the highest quality of service.

I-3B.2—To do nothing that diminishes the reputation of the program in which we work unless it is violating laws and regulations designed to protect children or the provisions of this Code.

Principles:

P-3B.1—When we do not agree with program policies, we shall first attempt to effect change through constructive action within the organization.

P-3B.2—We shall speak or act on behalf of an organization only when authorized. We shall take care to acknowledge when we are speaking for the organization and when we are expressing a personal judgment.

P-3B.3—We shall not violate laws or regulations designed to protect children and shall take appropriate action consistent with this Code when aware of such violations.

C—Responsibilities to employees

Ideals:

I-3C.1—To promote policies and working conditions that foster mutual respect, competence, well-being, and positive self-esteem in staff members.

I-3C.2—To create a climate of trust and candor that will enable staff to speak and act in the best interests of children, families, and the field of early childhood care and education.

I-3C.3—To strive to secure equitable compensation (salary and benefits) for those who work with or on behalf of young children.

Principles:

P-3C.1—In decisions concerning children and programs, we shall appropriately utilize the education, training, experience, and expertise of staff members.

P-3C.2—We shall provide staff members with safe and supportive working conditions that permit them to carry out their responsibilities, timely and nonthreatening evaluation procedures, written grievance procedures, constructive feedback, and opportunities for continuing professional development and advancement.

P-3C.3—We shall develop and maintain comprehensive written personnel policies that define program standards and, when applicable, that specify the extent to which employees are accountable for their conduct outside the workplace. These policies shall be given to new staff members and shall be available for review by all staff members.

P-3C.4—Employees who do not meet program standards shall be informed of areas of concern and, when possible, assisted in improving their performance.

P-3C.5—Employees who are dismissed shall be informed of the reasons for their termination. When a dismissal is for cause, justification must be based on evidence of inadequate or inappropriate behavior that is accurately documented, current, and available for the employee to review.

P-3C.6—In making evaluations and recommendations, judgments shall be based on fact and relevant to the interests of children and programs.

P-3C.7—Hiring and promotion shall be based solely on a person's record of accomplishment and ability to carry out the responsibilities of the position.

P-3C.8—In hiring, promotion, and provision of training, we shall not participate in any form of discrimination based on race, ethnicity, religion, gender, national origin, culture, disability, age, or sexual preference. We shall be familiar with and observe laws and regulations that pertain to employment discrimination.

Section IV: Ethical responsibilities to community and society

Early childhood programs operate within a context of an immediate community made up of families and other institutions concerned with children's welfare. Our responsibilities to the community are to provide programs that meet its needs, to cooperate with agencies and professions that share responsibility for children, and to develop needed programs that are not currently available. Because the larger society has a measure of responsibility for the welfare and protection of children, and because of our specialized expertise in child development, we acknowledge an obligation to serve as a voice for children everywhere.

Ideals:

I-4.1—To provide the community with high-quality (age and individually appropriate, and culturally and socially sensitive) education/care programs and services.

I-4.2—To promote cooperation among agencies and interdisciplinary collaboration among professions concerned with the welfare of young children, their families, and their teachers.

I-4.3—To work, through education, research, and advocacy, toward an environmentally safe world in which all children receive adequate health care, food, and shelter, are nurtured, and live free from violence.

I-4.4—To work, through education, research, and advocacy, toward a society in which all young children have access to high-quality education/care programs.

I-4.5—To promote knowledge and understanding of young children and their needs. To work toward greater social acknowledgment of children's rights and greater social acceptance of responsibility for their well being.

I-4.6—To support policies and laws that promote the well-being of children and families, and to oppose those that impair their well-being. To participate in developing policies and laws that are needed, and to cooperate with other individuals and groups in these efforts.

I-4.7—To further the professional development of the field of early childhood care and education and to strengthen its commitment to realizing its core values as reflected in this Code.

Principles:

P-4.1—We shall communicate openly and truthfully about the nature and extent of services that we provide.

P-4.2—We shall not accept or continue to work in positions for which we are personally unsuited or professionally unqualified. We shall not offer services that we do not have the competence, qualifications, or resources to provide.

P-4.3—We shall be objective and accurate in reporting the knowledge upon which we base our program practices.

P-4.4—We shall cooperate with other professionals who work with children and their families.

P-4.5—We shall not hire or recommend for employment any person whose competence, qualifications, or character makes him or her unsuited for the position.

P-4.6—We shall report the unethical or incompetent behavior of a colleague to a supervisor when informal resolution is not effective.

P-4.7—We shall be familiar with laws and regulations that serve to protect the children in our programs.

P-4.8—We shall not participate in practices which are in violation of laws and regulations that protect the children in our programs.

P-4.9—When we have evidence that an early childhood program is violating laws or regulations protecting children, we shall report it to persons responsible for the program. If compliance is not accomplished within a reasonable time, we will report the violation to appropriate authorities who can be expected to remedy the situation.

P-4.10—When we have evidence that an agency or a professional charged with providing services to children, families, or teachers is failing to meet its obligations, we acknowledge a collective ethical responsibility to report the problem to appropriate authorities or to the public.

P-4.11—When a program violates or requires its employees to violate this Code, it is permissible, after fair assessment of the evidence, to disclose the identity of that program.

APPENDIX B: DEC CODE OF ETHICS

CODE OF ETHICS

The Division for Early Childhood of the Council for Exceptional Children

Adopted: September, 1996

Revised: April, 1999

As members of the Division for Early Childhood (DEC) of the Council for Exceptional Children (CEC), we recognize that in our professional conduct we are faced with choices that call on us to determine right from wrong. Other choices, however, are not nearly as clear, forcing us to choose between competing priorities and to acknowledge the moral ambiguity of life. The following code of ethics is based on the Division's recognition of the critical role of conscience, not merely in preventing wrong, but in choosing among courses of action in order to act in the best interests of young children with special needs and their families and to support our professional colleagues.

As members of DEC, we acknowledge our responsibility to abide by high standards of performance and ethical conduct and we commit to:

1. Demonstrate the highest standards of personal integrity, truthfulness, and honesty in all our professional activities in order to inspire the confidence and trust of the public and those with whom we work;

2. Demonstrate our respect and concern for children and families, colleagues, and others with whom we work, honoring their beliefs, values, customs, and culture;

3. Demonstrate our respect for families in their task of nurturing their children and support them in achieving the outcomes they desire for themselves and their children;

4. Demonstrate, in our behavior and language, that we respect and appreciate the unique value and human potential of each child;

5. Strive for personal professional excellence, seeking new information, using new information and ideas, and responding openly to the suggestions of others;

6. Encourage the professional development of our colleagues and those seeking to enter fields related to early childhood special education, early intervention, and personnel preparation, offering guidance, assistance, support, and mentorship to others without the burden of professional competition;

7. Ensure that programs and services we provide are based on law as well as current knowledge of and recommended practice in early childhood special education, early intervention, and personnel preparation;

8. Serve as an advocate for children with special needs and their families and for the professionals who serve them in our communities working with those who make the policy and programmatic decisions that enhance or depreciate the quality of their lives;

9. Oppose any discrimination because of race, color, religion, sex, sexual orientation, national origin, political affiliation, disability, age, or marital status in all aspects of personnel action and service delivery;

10. Protect the privacy and confidentiality of information regarding children and families, colleagues, and students; and

11. Reflect our commitment to the Division for Early Childhood and to its adopted policies and positions.

The Division for Early Childhood acknowledges with appreciation the National Association for the Education of Young Children, the American Society for Public Administration, and the Council for Exceptional Children, whose codes of conduct were helpful as we developed our own.

Permission to copy not required - distribution encouraged

2

PERSPECTIVES ON HISTORY AND THEORY

The principal goal of education is to create men who are capable of doing new things, not simply of repeating what other generations have done.

Jean Piaget (1896–1980)

▼ *Chapter Objectives*

After reading this chapter, you should be able to:

- ▼ Identify significant leaders in early childhood education.
- ▼ Understand the major ideas and contributions to early childhood education of history's most important figures.

As you think about and apply chapter content on your own, you should be able to:

- ▼ Continue to formulate your own philosophy of early childhood education, with more awareness of the original sources of your thinking.
- ▼ Observe elements of historical influence in various early childhood settings.

When you look at a young child, what do you see? Surely your interest in pursuing a career in early childhood education means that you see beyond outward appearances: an open smile, an adorable outfit, a charmingly awkward pose. If you think of yourself as a teacher of this child, do you see a small being waiting eagerly for you to share the knowledge that you have gained over the years? Or do you see someone who will learn best if allowed to remain independent, with you as an occasional guide? Do you see this child as innately good but in danger of losing that goodness within a hostile environment? Or do you see a child born neutral, ready to soak up the social environment as a sponge might?

All these views, and many more, have been held by large groups of adults at different times in history. At times, the welfare of children and their educational needs have been of great concern; at other times, they seem to have been scarcely considered. For much of history, attitudes on children and education were simply taken for granted, and change came slowly. Today, however, much research and thought are devoted to child development and early education. This doesn't mean that definitive answers have been found to questions about what children are and what they need to develop most adequately. It does mean that to be effective, we cannot simply take children's development for granted. The world is changing too fast, with more and more demands on children to perform at higher intellectual and physical levels. As teachers, we need to be aware of what these pressures do to children and to help them develop in the best ways possible.

One way to become more aware of our own attitudes and beliefs is to learn more about their roots. To do this, we must look back at key figures in history for what we think today is part of an intellectual tradition that dates from antiquity.

SOME ANCIENT HISTORY

The centuries of prehistory are, of course, unknown to us, but we can safely assume that the education of young children during this period was directly related to survival issues and was nearly always the responsibility of the same-sex parent. Teaching techniques were probably quite simple and direct. We can relate to this method, for example, when we take a child out for her first walk in the woods. Since there may be poisonous plants and dangerous areas to avoid, we depend on simple instructions rather than hands-on discovery learning. Thus, in survival situations, we still retain a close kinship to our ancient ancestors.

Once beyond the survival level of instruction, however, we can begin thinking about what else children might need or want to learn and how we might best teach them. To look at the oldest recorded thoughts on early education, we turn first to the ideas of the Greek philosopher Plato and then move on to the Romans and the early Christians. At this point, you may wonder why we appear to ignore philosophies from other parts of the world. Our reason, quite simply, is that the cultures we discuss are those that still influence the way we view and teach children here in the United States.

The Early Greeks

So, let us begin with Plato (427?–347 B.C.), who, in the fourth century B.C., could look at and respond to a fairly well-developed educational system and comment on the status of childhood itself. Although the Greek view of infants and young children varied from state to state, infanticide was a universal practice, particularly in regard to girls and infants with birth defects. At best, an unwanted infant might be "potted," that is, put in a pot or basket and left at a temple gate in hopes that someone who needed a servant might adopt it. As Lloyd deMause (1974) noted, "The further back in history one goes, the lower the level of child care, and the more likely children are to be killed, abandoned, beaten, terrorized, and sexually abused" (p. 1).

It is interesting to compare the treatment of young children as demonstrated in two city–states of that time, Sparta and Athens. In Sparta, education began at about age 6 and was probably available only to boys. Prior to that, boys might attend their fathers' club meetings and play informal games that involved stealing food off the table without getting caught. This was lighthearted training for the serious business of learning to wage war and keep down rebellions. The more serious education began at about the time we would send a boy off to elementary school, but in this case the sole purpose was to train warriors for the state. Boys were put into gangs, given scant provisions, and sent off to forage in any way they could; even murder was sanctioned. Girls were given training at home for domestic life, but they might also be provided with quasi-military training to prepare them to be wives and mothers of state warriors.

It was not to the Spartans that Plato wrote his philosophical views, however, but to the Athenians at a time when their government was in some disarray. In the context of describing the ideal state, Plato suggested a design for early childhood education. From birth to age 6, learning should be informal, for "knowledge which is acquired under compulsion obtains no hold on the mind. So do not use compulsion, but let early education be a sort of amusement" (Gwynne-Thomas, 1981, p. 14). Good health and good social habits were to be inculcated by attentive parents who would provide plenty of close supervision; freedom was only to be earned over time.

For boys old enough to start school (at about age 6), Plato argued that the racier stories about the gods should be cleaned up and presented in a more ideal fashion to impressionable young minds. His enthusiasm for musical training also came with reservations, and he suggested that music be chosen that would promote the right attitudes, particularly toward the state.

It should be pointed out that Plato's ideas about education were tied to an ideal republic that could only function successfully with a large slave class. In fact, the word *pedagogue* is almost identical to the Greek word for slave–teacher: an educated person, enslaved by victors of a battle, assigned as a child's tutor and companion.

Aristotle (384–322 B.C.), like his teacher and mentor Plato, believed that early education was important. He argued that children have varying talents and skills, and that these should be enhanced. Thus he may be the first writer to recognize the educational importance of individual differences (Osborn, 1980).

The Early Romans

The inability of the Greek states to stop warring among themselves eventually led to their downfall, as Roman armies conquered them one by one. Once again, many educated Greeks found themselves in the role of teacher–slave, this time to the eager-to-learn Romans. Until their rise to power, Roman thought was considerably less sensitive, inventive, and curious than the Greeks'. Roman education was restricted to the basic necessities of life: fighting, farming, swimming, and riding, for example. There was little to read except for the rules of the state gathered in "The Laws of the Twelve Tables," published in 450 B.C. Greek influence changed all that.

Perhaps the best known and most influential Greco-Roman thinker was Quintilian (A.D. 35–97). Born in Spain but educated in Rome, Quintilian felt that in order to produce young adults of good character, education must begin at the age of 1. Responsible parents and tutors, as well as carefully chosen companions, were important because they set examples for impressionable youngsters. And examples were important in the development of character and speech patterns. According to Quintilian, what the child learned while young and still at home would have lifelong implications.

Quintilian recommended making lessons as interesting as possible. Encouragement should come from the use of praise and never from corporal punishment. Academics should be balanced with gymnastic training, Quintilian said, in order to promote health.

Rome's overexpansion eventually made it impossible for it to keep all its territories fortified and under control. As new groups of less educated outsiders began to conquer Roman territories, education began to decline, until much of the learning of the past centuries was all but lost. Many centuries later it would be "found" again and recognized as the basis of some of the same issues we write about and discuss today. Regarding early childhood education in particular, we can look back to Plato for his argument for informal learning and freedom based on structured guidance. Today's controversies about appropriate literature and music for children were also considered by Plato. For the recognition of individual differences, we can look to Aristotle. And for role modeling and positive reinforcement through praise (vs. corporal punishment), there is Quintilian. That these positive ideals should have been lost from the mid-5th to the 11th century and beyond was definitely a setback in the education of young children.

The Early Christians

By the middle of the 5th century A.D., the Roman Empire had officially collapsed, and new struggles for control took place. Most notable was the Christian church's rise to power. Earlier this had worked in favor of young children, since the newborn was deemed the owner of a soul, and infanticide was considered murder and punishable. The Christian emperor Constantine made killing a child a crime in 318, and by the next century there were stipends provided to families that kept foundlings and orphans. In 313 Constantine decreed Christianity the official religion of the Roman Empire, and Christian schools spread throughout much of Europe.

With the fall of the Roman Empire, the influence of the Christian church began to be increasingly anti-intellectual. Fewer and fewer people were educated, and the newly emerging monasteries became the principal repositories of knowledge. Even there, however, intellectual freedom was highly constrained. For example, one monk who tried to translate all of Plato and Aristotle from the Greek to Latin was sentenced to die for his "crime." Over the next 5 centuries, few children received an education: only those who planned to enter the monastery and those who belonged to wealthy families. As convents arose, girls were occasionally educated, particularly in what is now Germany.

The prevailing view of young children, what they were and what should be done with them, changed gradually from the Greek, Roman, and early Christian attitudes. As the concept of original sin took hold in religious thought, children came to be seen as inherently evil, thus condoning punishments that today we would define as child abuse. Furthermore, the concept of childhood itself changed. As soon as children had outgrown the most helpless stages of infancy, they joined in the general adult life, both for work and play.

It was for later generations to term these centuries (from the Fall of Rome to the rebirth of Greek and Roman ideas) the Middle or Dark Ages. The people who lived through this period knew little, if anything, about better times. But better times did come, and with them new interpretations of the ancient ideas that provide the foundation for today's views of early education.

The onset of the Renaissance (from the Latin meaning *rebirth*) was very good news for young children. During the Middle Ages physical and sexual abuse had been widespread, even condoned by some of the great philosophers and religious thinkers. Although infanticide had been given up, it was still a difficult time for children, as some form of abandonment seemed the prime alternative to murder. The wet nurse, monastery, convent, and foster family were all acceptable avenues of abandonment, and infanticide still persisted, although it was more covert. For example, an unusually large number of babies were reported to have died while sleeping with their parents, who allegedly "laid over" the babies and smothered them. In addition, wet nurses could be paid to have an "accident." The beginning of the Renaissance produced an increasing number of child instruction manuals, demonstrating a new view of children that could only be an improvement on the previous centuries. These manuals and other writings show a new understanding of children's needs and identities as being separate from those of adults.

THE ROOTS OF TODAY'S VIEWS ON EARLY CHILDHOOD EDUCATION

Whereas the Middle Ages gave us no educational leaders in the field of early childhood education, later centuries did. Like ancient Greek and Roman philosophers, influential thinkers wrote about their ideas so that today we can look back and evaluate them. The Moravian John Amos Comenius (Jan Amos Komensky) was the first to posit a complete system of education in the style of Plato. By the time he did, however, much Renaissance thinking had been altered by the period of religious Reformation.

John Comenius

John Amos Comenius (Jan Amos Komensky in the original Czech, 1592–1670) was a bishop in the persecuted Moravian church who spent most of his adult life in exile. Nevertheless, his educational ideas were widely received throughout Europe, his books were translated into more than a dozen languages, and he was invited by several European governments to reconstruct their educational systems. In succeeding centuries he was sometimes forgotten, and that is surely now the case. Yet if any thinker was responsible for pulling education, including early childhood education, out of the Middle Ages, it was Comenius. Here are some of the things he said in his book *School of Infancy* (1633/1896), which dealt with children to age 6. Note how closely his ideas fit with our own. For example, a major issue in early education today is developmental appropriateness in children's learning. This concept comes directly from Comenius. He understood that younger children are best able to grasp knowledge that relates to their own lives and that learning must be concrete before it can be abstract.

Today the study of history typically begins with the here and now and, as children grow older, adds on previous centuries. It was Comenius who first observed that young children need help in simply understanding yesterday and tomorrow and that they need to do this before trying to comprehend last year and beyond. Geography is another of the social studies influenced by Comenius. He realized that just as children first understand time in terms of today, they first understand space in relation to what they can see around themselves. Thus, he argued that geography should begin with the study of familiar places. Science study also begins with what is nearest and dearest to young children: nature. Again, this idea originated with Comenius. His views on arithmetic appear in today's textbooks and lesson plans, too. He suggested that young children, should begin by learning such basic concepts as *a lot* or *a little*. Although he said that small children could learn to count, he added that it would take several years for them to understand numbers. Research done in recent decades has proven him completely right. In this, as in so many other instances, Comenius was far ahead of his time. Perhaps that is one reason that at a practical level his educational ideas were not as widespread as his popularity might indicate. But it is his ideas that affected later educational thinkers, some of whom we discuss in this chapter.

John Locke

An English philosopher of the following century, John Locke (1632–1704) was brought up in a Puritan family, but his adult thinking was more influenced by the scientific revolution than by Reformation Protestant thinking. At Oxford he studied and later taught Greek, rhetoric, and moral philosophy. In his mid-30s Locke's more practical and scientific nature eventually led him back to the university to study medicine. He never succeeded in getting his terminal degree and only practiced medicine a short while, but the balance between the scientific and the philosophical in Locke's thinking and education produced a like balance in his later writing on education. While working as the personal secretary to the earl of Shaftesbury and tutoring the earl's son, he began to formulate his views on education, which, along with his anti-authoritarian political ideas, were revolutionary for their time. The only major work on education published during Locke's lifetime was *Some Thoughts Concerning Education*, and this was not originally intended as a book for the public. A cousin and her husband asked Locke to write some letters giving advice on the upbringing of their son, and these were eventually published in book form. All Locke's philosophical and medical thinking, as well as his past experiences, went into these letters. So did his views on social class. His cousin's son was to be raised as a gentleman, and Locke differentiated the education of a future gentleman from that of a commoner's child. Thus, despite his increasing involvement in the politics of the Enlightenment, Locke did not propose the kind of universal education that Comenius did.

Nonetheless, Locke's ideas on early education represented new ways of looking at children and formed the basis for much of what we think and do today. His view of infants was that they are born with great potential for learning. Their minds, he said, might be viewed as white paper or an empty cabinet or a blank tablet. What they become as adults is then defined by their total education: "I think I may say that of all the men we meet with, nine parts of ten are what they are, good or evil, useful or not, by their education" (Locke, 1692/1910, p. 9).

Another idea that set Locke apart from the educational thinkers of his day was his belief that in educating children we need to be aware of individual differences:

> There is a difference of degree in men's understandings, apprehensions, and reasonings to so great a latitude . . . that there is a greater distance between some men and others in this respect, than between some men and some beasts. (Cleverley & Phillips, 1986, p. 18)

This concept is contrast to the prevailing idea that there was a general mass of knowledge out there to be learned, and everyone in a group or class should move along together in conquering it. For Locke, our minds might all begin as blank slates, but some slates are higher quality than others. In other words, Locke (1692/1910) did not completely dismiss heredity and even said:

> God has stamped certain characters upon men's minds, which, like their shapes, may perhaps be a little mended, but can hardly be totally altered and transformed into the contrary. (p. 43)

For young children, Locke (1692/1910) wrote in favor of play and freedom, but he also supported disciplined living and even some deprivation for upper-class children, who were, in his view, overly pampered. Although his ideas along this line were sometimes contradictory, Locke was consistent in arguing for a positive approach to both teaching and discipline:

> Beating then, and all other sorts of slavish and corporal punishments, are not the discipline fit to be used in the education of those who would have wise, good, and ingenuous men; and therefore very rarely to be applied, and that only on great occasions, and cases of extremity. (p. 39)

What Locke did advocate when discipline was necessary was stern, disapproving looks as well as shaming. To keep children from getting too spoiled, as well as to promote rugged health, he suggested cold foot baths, open air, loose fitting clothing and not much of it, a simple diet, and a hard bed. He may be the first educational philosopher to discuss toilet training, and on this subject he maintained his stern view, recommending regular visits with enforced sitting. For Locke (1692/1910), "A sound mind in a sound body is a short, but full description of a happy state in the world" (p. 9)

Much of Locke's thinking pervades early childhood education today, although the form it takes in practice may be much altered. As an example, consider his view that individuals are born like blank slates but that they may differ qualitatively. For Locke, this meant the permanent subjugation of some classes of people. Today, although there are those who believe as he did, we generally argue that this attitude is potentially racist, sexist, classist, or prejudiced in some other way. At the same time, it is possible to accommodate Locke's view of the blank slate in an updated, more democratic approach to teaching children from all walks of life.

When Locke said that the environment would create the child, he referred to its entire intellectual, social, and physical entity. Full learning experiences should involve input from all these aspects of the environment and include the child's use of all the senses: When you see a classroom with much opportunity for learning through acting on sensory materials, you may well be observing a classroom whose roots go back to Locke's 17th-century views. For the materials to be truly Lockean, however, they must have a learning goal connected to them. Locke believed that the environment should be controlled so that children learn what they should know. Some examples of what you might observe today would be math games using concrete materials, cardboard cut-out letters used in creating simple words, or perhaps wooden puzzles; all of these are sensory and all have specific learning goals.

Today's behaviorist psychology also owes some portion of its basic thinking to Locke. One of Locke's views was that children should be reinforced for their good behavior and intellectual successes. Little is accomplished, he argued, by approaching a child with a negative attitude or physical punishment. These should be saved for emergency cases. At the same time, Locke believed that too much reinforcement could have the wrong effect, making a child more demanding and spoiled, refusing to do schoolwork unless rewarded. Today's behaviorists have created classroom approaches to discipline that are much like those that Locke would have recommended. Reinforcements are positive, focus on negative behavior is avoided, and rewards are gradually withdrawn as behavior or performance improves. Since teacher behavior is usually more subtle to observe than learning materials, you may have to look longer and more carefully to see these influences from Locke. It may be nothing more than a carefully timed, "You worked hard at that, didn't you?" or the old standby, "I like the way Emily and Al are sitting," but these and other similar statements have a direct effect on children's attitudes and behaviors. Watch for them.

Jean Jacques Rousseau

Jean Jacques Rousseau (1712–1778), born in Switzerland not long after Locke died, combined philosophical and educational thought in his writings as Locke had done. Like Locke, he was an influential force for egalitarianism and democracy in his soci-

Locke and Rousseau proposed different views of early education based on different views of human learning. Locke saw children's minds as blank slates or empty buckets to be filled by the teachings of knowledgeable adults. Rousseau, however, saw children's minds as naturally programmed to unfold in their own way and at their own pace if given a secure environment by nurturing adults.

ety, but the conclusions he reached were different enough from those of Locke to inspire a very different form of early education.

In some ways it is difficult to believe that someone of Rousseau's background could affect both politics and education in the intense ways that he did. His mother died while giving birth to him, and his father first spoiled and then deserted him. He was passed around among relatives and received little education, although by age 10 he had read countless novels. Apprenticed to an engraver, Rousseau tired of the cruel treatment he received and ran away. He began the life of a wanderer, trying various occupations (clerk, secretary, music copyist, even priest) and usually failing. At age 27 Rousseau was hired as a tutor to two young boys. He lasted just about a year, failing miserably at disciplining them in any way. But by now the wanderer was in France, where he became involved in society and numerous love affairs, in particular with one woman from the lower class who became his lifelong companion (he eventually married her when in his 60s) and who bore him five children. All of these he abandoned to a foundling home.

How, then, did Rousseau manage to influence his own and future generations in two major fields, politics and child development? As one author (Wodehouse, 1924) explained it, the enlightened gentlemen of the age of Locke were ready for new influences, something of a more "natural" condition and, "about 1760, a few books connected with this subject struck the general imagination with extraordinary force. They came from a somewhat lower cosmopolitan level, being the work of a rather disreputable Swiss from Geneva, living in France, who happened to have genius" (p. 101).

In his major work on education published in 1762, *Emile*, Rousseau seemed to idealize the details of his own life in the fictional biography of a "perfectly" brought up and educated boy. Was Rousseau abandoned as a child, and did he abandon his own children? He could turn that into a positive experience for Emile, who would be given freedom to roam, play, and follow his spontaneous impulses. About this Rousseau wrote, "What is to be thought of that cruel education . . . that burdens a child with all sorts of restrictions and begins by making him miserable, in order to prepare him for some far-off happiness which he may never enjoy?" (Weber, 1984, p. 27).

The force of Rousseau's thought was much stronger than the details of his often sordid life. Let's take a look at some of his ideas on early childhood education because they eventually gave rise to many of the ideas we practice today.

Rousseau argued that early childhood education should come from all the senses, and that reading should not be pushed. In fact, he felt that it would be better for a child not to read at all until about age 12. The teacher or tutor should not use direct instruction but should act as a guide. The teacher should be aware of the child's interests and let him follow those interests rather than prescribe a curriculum. Discipline should be primarily through the natural consequences of the child's actions. Much of the child's education should take place outdoors, and emphasis should be placed on healthful development. One of Rousseau's views of the child set him apart from the traditional religious thinkers: Where they saw the infant as inherently evil, Rousseau saw him as basically good. "God makes all things good; man meddles with them and they become evil" (Weber, 1984, p. 27). Thus, the general approach in the education of a young child was to tuck him safely away from the world in a protected environment where the only influences were those of good.

We should note that Rousseau's ideal education was reserved for children of the middle and upper classes. Like Locke, he believed that little education was needed for the lower classes. In Rousseau's case, this could be justified by his idea of naturalism, in which the child is educated by his surroundings. The poor, he decided, could take care of what little education they needed right where they were. In *Emile*, Rousseau also revealed his attitude toward women:

[Women are] specially made to please men, he said, to be useful to them, to make themselves loved and honored by them, to rear them when young, to care for them when grown up, to advise them, to console them, to render their lives, agreeable and sweet to them—these are the duties of women at all times, and should be taught to them from their childhood. . . . It is a law of nature that woman shall obey man. (Compayre, 1907, p. 84)

This was the "natural" woman who would be the helpmate of the free and unspoiled "natural" man.

Rousseau's ideas on education were complemented by his thoughts on politics. Much of what he wrote influenced antiroyalist thinkers and helped bring on the French Revolution, which he did not live to see. Occasionally, some progressive fathers of his century and the next actually tried Rousseau's ideas on their own little Emiles, generally with disastrous results. He did not live to see this either, as his ideas on both politics and education had more effect after his death.

Today, you are as likely to see Rousseau's influences in the classroom as you are Locke's. Again, you can observe children interacting actively with materials that appeal to all their senses. But, in keeping with the concept of natural development, the materials are more open-ended and their use determined by the children. Math materials might be sticks brought inside by the children. These could be played with in a free-form way, while the teacher makes informal comments to inspire learning. Books might or might not be available, and the teacher could well choose to tell a story rather than read it. Giving children materials for costumes and props so that they might invent little plays would take preference over providing structured reading. Time spent outdoors would focus on learning about nature in an informal way.

A basic difference between Locke and Rousseau affects what you see in the classroom today. Along with others of his time, Locke assumed that there is a discreet body of knowledge that people of the upper classes should learn and that the function of education is to make knowledge accessible and interesting. Rousseau, on the other hand, was more interested in process, or learning how to learn. You can observe this difference in outlook when you see children playing with materials that have right solutions (Locke's view) or when you see them playing with open-ended materials, creating their own learning (Rousseau's view). In most classrooms you will find some of each kind of learning, living testament to our inability to decide which is the better course to take. Many teachers argue that a combination of the two views provides the best learning, although many of them aren't aware that their argument is based on a conflict in ideology that has been around for more than two centuries.

Just as Locke's ideas were modified by succeeding generations, so were Rousseau's. Parents who took his ideas literally found themselves creating ill-mannered, self-centered, illiterate adolescents. Still, his ideas offered inspiration for more practical interpreters. In Rousseau's native Switzerland, a man of the next generation molded his ideas into a more useful form and succeeded in educating children in a more natural way than ever before.

Johann Pestalozzi

Johann Heinrich Pestalozzi (1746–1827), like Rousseau, had an unhappy childhood. Born into a comfortably affluent family, his whole life changed at the age of 5, when his father died. He was subsequently brought up by his mother and a family servant. Pestalozzi had a delicate constitution, and his apparently odd appearance and personality made him the object of other children's jokes. Even in his later years, commentators referred to his peculiar personality.

His motives in life were tied from his early years to the fate of the downtrodden. Like Locke and Rousseau before him, he was politically attuned to the need for some democratization in his country. Unlike them, he was sympathetic to the needs and deprivations of the poorer classes. As a young man he married and settled on a farm, having been inspired by his readings of Rousseau to seek the "natural" life. Soon he was providing a home for some 20 orphans and poor children. His poor business management ensured that he would eventually fail at the effort, but within a short time Pestalozzi published a successful novel, *Leonard and Gertrude* in 1781–1787, which

Among the enduring contributions of Pestalozzi were his insistence on universal education for both the rich and the poor of both sexes and for early learning that moves from the concrete to the abstract through the use of manipulative materials.

made him famous and gave him some income. It contained his views on education, which were influenced by his earlier reading of Rousseau's *Emile*. In one important respect, however, he took issue with Rousseau. To Pestalozzi, unlimited freedom would not bring children to the desired educational level. In Pestalozzi's view, "liberty is a good thing, obedience is equally so" (Gwynne-Thomas, 1981, p. 235).

In 1799, Napoleon invaded Switzerland and, after sacking the town of Stanz, left hundreds of children destitute. An orphanage was established with Pestalozzi in charge. There he was able to put into practice the domestic love, emotional stability, and sensory education he had been writing about. Although the French eventually returned and commandeered the orphanage for a military hospital, Pestalozzi's life career was begun. By 1805 he had established a school in the town of Yverdon, which, for 20 years, was an internationally known model of the latest in education.

In his school, Pestalozzi took Rousseau's basic ideas about natural education, freedom, sensory learning, and so on, and made them work. Rousseau had escaped his own life by writing about a fictional ideal; Pestalozzi chose not to deny his own experience but to use it to empathize with and help others. Although his writings were well known, it was his ability to put his ideas into practice that gave Pestalozzi his lasting fame.

Much of what Pestalozzi did and recommended still influences what we do with young children today. He believed then, as most of us do today, that poor children have as much right to education as their wealthier counterparts. In fact, it was Pestalozzi's intention to attempt a real elevation of their lives. Additionally, he matter of factly included girls in his educational plans, a radical departure from tradition. Although he believed in equal access to education for everyone, he also valued diversity, saying, "Idiosyncracies of the individual are the greatest blessings of nature and must be respected to the highest degree" (Weber, 1984, p. 29).

In the classroom, Pestalozzi geared experiences so that they went from the concrete to the abstract, a major innovation for his time. For the younger children there were "object lessons," what we might call manipulative materials, that gave children their first understanding of form, language, and number. The order, he said, would be to "steadily increase the range of their practical experience with things"; then the teacher would "do all that is possible to clear this experience from confusion and indefiniteness." Finally, when the concrete lesson was clear, the teacher would "supply them with words . . . going, indeed, a little farther in preparation for the future" (Pestalozzi, 1912, p. 93).

Today we describe Pestalozzi's choice of natural, concrete materials as developmentally appropriate for young children. He also saw these materials as a way to interest young children in school. In his best-known book, *How Gertrude Teaches Her Children* (1801), Pestalozzi remarked at length on the wonderful freedom of preschool children and decried what traditionally happened to them once they attended school:

> [S]uddenly, after five years of blissful sensuous life, we banish all Nature from their eyes . . . we herd them together like sheep in an evil-smelling room; for hours, days, weeks, months, and years, we chain them unmercifully to the contemplation of miserable and monotonously unexciting alphabets, and condemn them to an existence which, in comparison with their former life, is repulsive in the extreme. . . . (Pestalozzi, p. 89)

In actual practice, Pestalozzi did not always live up to his own ideals. In extreme cases he might resort to corporal punishment, and sometimes his ideas about object lessons gave way to boring drills that he somehow convinced himself the children loved, despite the obvious agony visitors observed on their faces.

Today we can see both sides of Pestalozzi in action: the use of manipulative materials juxtaposed with drill materials that seem to get the job done faster and with fewer frustrations—at least for the adult. The latter approach, however, is not an example of Pestalozzi's thinking but of the normal adult's occasional impatience with children. Let us focus instead on his ideas that are still philosophically sound. Pestalozzi developed activities and materials that encouraged children to learn from the concrete to the abstract. If you observe first in a nursery school and then in a third grade you will, no doubt, see this developmental sequence in action. Four-year-olds, who gain an intuitive understanding of division when they share crackers equally among the group, can later transmit that understanding to pencil-and-paper problems, as long as they have something concrete to help them understand.

Another enduring contribution was Pestalozzi's insistence on universal education. He believed that both rich and poor, boys and girls deserved to learn. The increasing democratization of Western thought made such a concept more acceptable than it had been in previous generations. Today, we take for granted the right to free education, although the equalization of quality is often problematic. Still, if you are female or have grown up poor, you owe your education, in part, to the groundwork laid by Pestalozzi.

It was the observations of his school at Yverdon that made Pestalozzi famous throughout the world. For early childhood education, it was the visit of the German educator Friedrich Froebel to the school that was most important. His experience there transformed Froebel from a rural schoolmaster into a theorist and philosopher.

Friedrich Froebel

Yet again, we have an example of an influential educator shaped by his own unhappy childhood. Friedrich Froebel's (1782–1852) mother died early in his life, and Froebel later wrote, "This loss, a hard blow to me, influenced the whole environment and development of my being: I consider that my mother's death decided more or less the external circumstances of my whole life" (Shapiro, 1983, p. 19). At the age of 15 he was apprenticed to a forester and began a lifelong attachment to nature. Perhaps it was this experience that contributed to his inability to stick with university studies and sent him off to work as a land surveyor, estate manager, forest department official, museum assistant, tutor, and, finally, rural school teacher.

Between 1808 and 1810, Froebel attended the training institute run by Pestalozzi at Yverdon. Although he came away accepting the basic principles of Pestalozzi's theories, Froebel felt that something critically important was missing: the "spiritual mechanism" that is the foundation of early learning. "Pestalozzi takes man existing only in his appearance on earth," he said, "but I take man in his eternal being, in his eternal existence" (Shapiro, 1983, p. 20). Froebel also rejected ideas, still popular with the followers of Rousseau, concerning education that was largely outdoors. Although he loved nature and wanted children to as well, he wanted to protect them from its more raw aspects.

Eventually, Froebel's concern for children's moral, spiritual, physical, and intellectual growth led him to focus on their needs just prior to entering school. He shared Pestalozzi's horror of what happened to 5-year-olds whose uninhibited, happy lives were so radically changed by their entrance into school. What Froebel envisioned was a sort of halfway house between home and school, infancy and childhood that would be attended by 4- to 6-year-olds. Because it would be a place where children were nurtured and protected from outside influences, much as plants might be in a garden, Froebel decided to call his school a *kinder* (children) *garten* (garden).

To make his kindergarten successful, Froebel knew that special teacher training would be necessary. He also decided that new concrete materials must be developed. They must be age appropriate for children's interests and have an underlying spiritual message. To meet the first need, Froebel began a training institute alongside his first school. For the second, he developed a series of play objects as well as singing games that seemed appropriate to the interests and education of young children and had a spiritual message as well.

The educational materials were divided into two groups: *gifts* and *occupations*. The first two gifts were designed to be introduced in infancy by the mother, and Froebel fully expected babies to have a beginning understanding of what they were about. For example, the first gift was a yarn ball connected to a string, which was to be played with under the mother's supervision in such a way that the baby's senses and muscles would be stimulated. But Froebel also believed that the ball would "awaken spirit and individuality" while helping the infant intuit "unity" (from the shape of the ball) and "freedom" (from its swinging motion). Three more gifts introduced to children in kindergarten were small building blocks that would fit together in prescribed ways under the teacher's instructions.

It is important to note here that Froebel considered these directed exercises with their specific goals a form of play. Compared to what most children in those days dealt with in their daily lives, it probably would have felt like very liberating play. Today, however, we would no doubt quibble that close-ended, prescribed, teacher-directed activities might be enjoyable but could not be described as play.

The occupations allowed children more freedom and included such things as weaving, bead-stringing, sewing, and stick-laying activities, as well as gardening. But even these held underlying spiritual messages that could be learned in such simple steps as the required and careful cleanup. This last step in every activity was considered "a final, concrete reminder to the child of God's plan for moral and social order" (Shapiro, 1983, p. 24). The essential harmony of the gifts and occupations had its counterpart in the songs and games that focused on social harmony. Break up a circle of children and you have an understanding of individuality; put it back together again and there is group unity. Teachers were to point out these symbolic acts to the children, and it was expected that the children would understand.

Froebel did not have the strong political inclinations of Locke, Rousseau, and Pestalozzi and, indeed, rejected political action as a way to achieve more rights for women, although it was a cause he championed. His definition of emancipation was that women would be permitted out of the home to teach. This may explain why one of his missions was to train women throughout the world in childrearing and teaching. Despite his rejection of politics, however, the Prussian government considered Froebel's ideas dangerous and ordered his schools closed in 1848. Despairing, he died 4 years later, not knowing that his educational ideas were about to take hold in the United States, bringing the still-new country an early education system unlike anything it had ever seen before.

The same Prussian repression and political rebellions that closed Froebel's kindergartens also sent numerous educated citizens out of the country, many of them to the United States. Among these were a number of women trained in the Froebel system of early education, and it was they who were responsible for introducing the kindergarten to this country. The very first kindergarten was established in Wisconsin for German immigrant children, who were taught in German. Word of this new way of teaching eventually made its way to St. Louis, where the first public kindergartens were opened. Although those responsible for establishing the schools were native-born Americans, they coupled Froebel's ideas with those of the German philosopher Hegel. Just as today there are people who worry about foreign influences altering the "American way," so there were concerns held by parents and educators then that early education in the United States was being taken over by German ideals. Despite this setback, Froebel's ideas provided the major direction that kindergartens followed during the last half of the 19th century. However, in a country that was beginning to look toward scientific theories rather than metaphysics and religion as a way to understand children, his ideas were gradually replaced by those of more scientific thinkers. The most radical of these eventually gained sufficient strength to be called the Child Study Movement.

One possible remaining influence that is unlike any other in our historical review is that the Froebel kindergarten has actually left its mark on the art and architecture of the 20th century. The brilliant architect Frank Lloyd Wright once claimed that playing with the Froebel gifts provided the foundation for his designs. Indeed, his mother spent much time at the demonstration Froebel kindergarten at the 1876 Centennial Exposition in Philadelphia, purchasing a collection of the materials for her young son and even taking a teacher-training course. One author argued that Wright was not alone in being influenced by his early experiences with the Froebel materials (Brosterman, 1997). He traced the styles of a number of well-known 20th century artists to their early kindergarten experiences.

To a large degree, Froebel remains forgotten today except in his role as the developer of the kindergarten. His belief that young children can understand the spiritual symbolism behind the games they play has been discarded. The rigidly structured use of play materials has been abandoned in most quarters. The finely detailed, perfectly measured and produced learning materials have been replaced by mass produced toys. Some things remain, however: the concept that children of preprimary years learn best through some form of play, the feeling that group games help children feel a part of the whole, the idea that playing and working outdoors can lead to creativity and good health. Froebel's ideas of natural learning and play demonstrated his debt to Rousseau, whereas the goal-oriented activities and materials followed the lead of Locke.

John Dewey

One of those responsible for the demise of Froebel's kindergarten movement was John Dewey (1859–1952). Born, raised, and educated in Vermont, Dewey graduated from the University of Vermont at the age of 20. He then spent 3 anxious months looking for work and more or less fell into teaching when a cousin offered him a job at the high school where he was principal. Dewey taught Latin, algebra, and science, but his reading and thinking leaned toward philosophy. One of his former philosophy professors encouraged him to publish, and he had immediate success with three articles. This encouraged him to pursue a doctorate in philosophy from Johns Hopkins University. He moved quickly up the academic ladder, going from professorships at the universities of Minnesota and Michigan to one at the University of Chicago in 1894. It was at Chicago that Dewey first gained national notice and respect for the application of his philosophical ideas to the education of children.

Dewey believed that children learn by doing and that participation in democratic decision making, whether in or out of school, develops rational problem-solving abilities and social skills.

As a young man, Dewey read the German philosopher Hegel and came to reject his ideas. This was important for his own later theories on early childhood education, because much of the symbolism in the activities, songs, and games of Froebel's kindergarten came from Hegel's philosophy. It was important, too, that Dewey went to the University of Chicago when he did, because both it and other institutions nearby were in the midst of exploring new ideas in education. Even Froebel kindergartens in the area were interested in innovation and were considered far too radical by their more orthodox counterparts.

University laboratory schools were a recent innovation, and Dewey was instrumental in beginning one at Chicago. It included a kindergarten as well as the elementary grades. In putting his theories of early education into action, Dewey found himself caught between two popular but antagonistic philosophies: that of Froebel, which he considered outdated and rigid, and that of the more recent Child Study Movement, which he believed had gone overboard in attempting to be scientific. In the mid-1890s, the followers of Froebel were a force to be reckoned with, so rather than striking out completely on his own, Dewey chose to reinterpret Froebel. As one example, he took Froebel's concept of unity (which we have seen expressed in children's circle games and in building blocks) and focused instead on unifying such concepts as *learning and doing,* and *child and society.* Learning and doing can be united if we consider that young children are constantly active and are enthusiastic about learning, leading us to conclude that perhaps children can and should learn by doing. Child and society are also two dissimilar concepts that can be united. The individual child can learn to be a part of society if the school itself becomes a microsociety.

In addition to his different interpretation of unity, Dewey's view on play was unlike that of Froebel's. Children at the experimental university school used the Froebel blocks but could play with them freely; no emphasis was put on observing the unity of the whole and the individuality of the separate pieces. Play was free, there was more of it, and the rigidly timed lessons disappeared entirely. Dewey's ideas on play came from the American philosopher and psychologist George Herbert Mead, who believed that play was grounded in a child's social environment. From this idea, Dewey developed a whole new way of structuring the school, from the earliest years on. No longer did children play with pretend or symbolic brooms and such. Instead, they really took care of their own classrooms, structuring them as minisocieties. Furthermore, Dewey believed that social development could best take place in classrooms with mixed ages. For him, the artificial divisions between grades were unnecessary and worked against children's social growth.

In the laboratory school, the subprimary classroom covered 2 years. To help the youngest children learn about society, teachers began with the already familiar home and the people in it. Bit by bit the outside world was then introduced. During the winter the children worked with Froebel building materials and arranged furniture and living spaces; in the spring they played outdoor games, studied nature, and took walks in the city. All the while, they played and worked with far more independence than children did in a Froebel kindergarten. Fostering democracy in the classroom was a major goal for Dewey and one of his most lasting contributions to education.

Dewey stayed at the University of Chicago 10 years and then moved on to Columbia University in New York. His interests branched into other areas, but his influence on early education has been lasting, although sometimes misinterpreted or unpopular. Misinterpretation was probably inevitable as Dewey's philosophical views were simplified and watered down in their widespread application. He believed that learning by doing was important, not just for kindergarten children but for older students as well. He was a proponent of teaching children of all ages about democracy by helping them create democratic societies in their classrooms. These ideas in the wrong hands and directed by teachers who read little, if any, of his philosophy could lead to the kind of classroom anarchy that Rousseau's early followers experienced. And that was just what happened. By the late 1940s, Dewey-inspired education was coming under widespread attack. By the late 1950s, when the weak nature of American education seemed exemplified in the Soviets' jumpstart into the space race, Dewey's philosophy was blamed. The backlash led to a greater focus on academics and eventually to a back-to-basics movement.

Of course, Dewey was never against academic learning. He believed, however, that children need to be actively involved in it and that academics should be meaningful to them. As the sterility of the back-to-basics approach became apparent, Dewey's ideas began to return. Today, as you see young children learn how to run town meetings in their classrooms, or observe a teacher who focuses on all aspects of children's growth, or learn to plan and teach a theme unit, you come in contact with education that has its roots in Dewey's thinking.

A bit younger than Dewey and on the other side of the Atlantic, Italy's first woman doctor was, at about the same time, developing an educational philosophy that might be placed somewhere between those of Froebel and Dewey.

Maria Montessori

Maria Montessori (1870–1952) was born in a small town on the Adriatic Sea in the same year that Italy succeeded in unifying its various independent states into one nation. The spirit of optimism in the new country gave hope to women and the poor, both traditionally downtrodden. Although this hope was eventually squashed by those who clung to tradition, it was sufficient during Montessori's youth to give her the boost she needed.

When she was 5 years old, the family moved to Rome. Her mother expected her to take an active interest in helping those less fortunate, so she knitted for the poor and befriended a hunchbacked girl in the neighborhood. As a young child in school, she performed only adequately, but in time she grew interested in math and technical subjects. With the help of her mother, she overcame her father's objections, and at age 13 entered the kind of technical school few Italian girls of her time dared enter. For a time she considered going on to study engineering, but she decided on medicine instead. This was totally unheard of for a woman, and when her father finally gave in, he insisted on accompanying her to class each day. As might be imagined, there was much prejudice against her presence, but she matched her courage with enthusiasm and brilliance and eventually graduated with high marks.

As a new doctor, some of her research took Montessori to the University of Rome's psychiatric clinic. There, amid insane adults, she saw large numbers of children with learning disabilities, placed there for lack of other choices. The inhumane treatment of these children touched her, and she began to read everything she could find on the education of the mentally handicapped. Eventually, she decided that there must be some way to reach these children and found herself influenced to some extent by Rousseau. Although she disagreed with his idea of unstructured education in the wilds of nature, she liked his idea of developing the senses before abstract learning takes place. She also studied the work of Pestalozzi and Froebel and adapted them to her own use.

Because Montessori wanted to help those who were termed "idiot" children, she also studied the writings of two French men who had pioneered work in that area, Jean Itard and Edouard Seguin. Itard, a doctor born a century before her, had gained international fame when he attempted to educate a young boy found running wild in the woods, "The Wild Child of Aveyron." Ultimately unsuccessful in his attempts, Itard still was inspired to continue looking for ways to treat other children with special cognitive needs or physical disabilities, particularly deafness.

Seguin, who studied with Itard, carried on the work, founding schools for those termed *idiots* both in France and in the United States. The unique methods he developed for educating children historically thought uneducable seemed to Montessori to hold promise for the children she observed locked up in insane asylums. She was convinced that it was education, not medicine, that would improve their lives. Soon she was speaking at conferences about the need to educate children with learning disabilities, and she proposed a school along Froebel's lines. Before long she found herself appointed director of a teacher-training institute that was a pioneer in the field of special education in Italy. Pulling her ideas from Froebel and others, Montessori experimented with teaching materials and activities, succeeding so well that her 8-year-old "defectives" eventually did as well as or better than normal children in state examinations for reading and writing.

For the next several years, Montessori moved back and forth between medicine and special education. During this time she developed a close relationship with one of her colleagues, gave birth to their son, and sent him off to the country to be raised by others. Only in his teens did she raise him herself, usually claiming that he was adopted or belonged to someone else (Kramer, 1976).

Meanwhile, Montessori was given the opportunity to test her educational ideas with children of normal intelligence when she was asked to start a day-care center in a new public housing project. Her success came quickly as she experimented with methods and materials, and international fame followed. Some of the school's attributes were born of necessity, then remained because of their effectiveness with children. Aspects of the so-called Children's House (Casa dei Bambini) that were new in that time and place were insufficient materials to go around (to foster sharing), mixed ages (to promote positive interrelationships), freedom of movement and child-choice of materials (to enhance self-direction and democracy), structured activities for the youngest and newest (to provide a sense of stability and confidence), and real tools for real work (to demonstrate respect for the children's abilities and to help them adjust to the real world).

Just as Pestalozzi's and Froebel's teacher-training institutes had attracted enthusiastic students from afar, so did Montessori's. Several Americans learned Italian for the purpose of attending, and in the early years of this century Montessori schools began to bloom in this country. Soon, however, they were denounced by influential scholars and for a time almost disappeared. You have, no doubt, noticed that there are Montessori schools today, however, and this is due to their rebirth in the late 1950s, when our society became newly concerned about academic learning for young children. The Montessori method, which encourages children to go as far as they can in their cognitive development, seemed to many an effective alternative for early childhood education.

Like Froebel, Maria Montessori did not live to see this resurgence of popularity in the United States. Her last years were spent largely in exile from Italy and its fascist dictator, Benito Mussolini. Her travels during World War II ensured the establishment of Montessori schools in India and the Netherlands. They also gave rise to her belief that if people, beginning in their early childhood, could have more learning and experience with democratic processes, they would be less likely to follow a Mussolini or a Hitler. It was a sentiment that no doubt would have been shared by John Dewey.

Montessori education has survived to this decade relatively intact. Although there are various approaches to training, with some purists wanting to keep the schools as they were in Montessori's day and others arguing for updating them, a common element is found in all the schools. If possible, you should try to observe at least one Montessori classroom. There, you will find a selection of materials designed to enhance learning through the senses, concrete math activities that help preschoolers intuit complex principles, and children moving independently and at will. It is likely that you will see little play in the free-form sense, and in this way, Montessori schools have a strong relationship to those of Froebel. Traditionally, Montessori schools have come under fire for their lack of creative experiences and free play. Responding to this criticism, many schools have added these elements to their programs, so you may find some differences if you observe in more than one place. In most Montessori schools there is some mixing of ages. The intent is to help the older children take responsibility for the younger while reinforcing their own learning, and for the younger children to learn to depend on and trust their older peers. Furthermore, the mixing of ages is designed to foster the creation of a predemocratic society, or "society in embryo," as Montessori referred to it.

In recent years, the Montessori philosophy has been grasped by those who want to give children an early academic push. This is an unfortunate interpretation of her belief that children should be given the freedom to go ahead in their learning if they so choose. Nevertheless, it fits with the growing trend for hurrying children along (Elkind, 1983). At approximately the same time that Montessori was beginning her children's house in Rome, a doctor and psychologist named Arnold Gesell was starting a much different trend in this country.

Arnold Gesell

Arnold Gesell (1880–1961) received his MD from Yale after completing a PhD in psychology at Clark University. For 30 years he carried on research at the Yale Clinic of Child Development, which had strong influences on childhood education, particularly for the early years. The roots of his thinking went back to Froebel, Pestalozzi, and Rousseau. Gesell's view of the child was related to that of a growing plant or tree or even an accreting coral. He believed that the seeds of adulthood are present from birth, and what is most needed for proper growth is simply proper watering and fertilizing. Gesell's thinking put the most emphasis on the idea of the unfolding, predetermined plant, but it also left room for the influence of the (less important) environment.

The psychological term that Gesell gave to this automatic unfoldment was *maturation*. Related to it was the educational term *readiness*. Observational research in the Yale laboratory suggested to Gesell that there were ages and stages to all aspects of growth: physical, emotional, mental, and school skills. His research led him to establish norms for many behaviors within these areas. For example, he observed that children were biologically ready to read when they had attained a mental age of 6½ years. The school skill of reading, therefore, has the following developmental norms:

15 months	Pats identified picture in book.
18 months	Points to an identified picture in book.
2 years	Names three pictures in book.
3 years	Identifies four printed geometric forms.

| 4 years | Recognizes salient capital letters. |
| 5 to 6 years | Recognizes salient printed words. (Weber, 1984, p. 57) |

To Gesell's way of thinking, a child who does not reach these behaviors according to schedule is not a candidate for pushing. His hands-off attitude was reminiscent of Rousseau's, as he argued the importance of waiting until a child demonstrates the appropriate readiness. Gesell's arguments were widely heard, and readiness became for many people in early education an important byword. Eventually he was taken to task by other psychological researchers, who noted that he had done his studies at the Yale Clinic of Child Development, where the children's parents were students and professors. In this privileged atmosphere, norms were established that were posited for the population as a whole. Gesell's detractors saw this lack of broad-based research and regard for environmental influences as the fatal flaw of his life's work. Furthermore, many have argued that the developmental schedules he established were too rigid and detailed to have universal application.

Nevertheless, Gesell's legacy lives on, and work continues at the Gesell Institute in Connecticut. In the 1970s, Louise Ames and others published *The Gesell Institute's Child from One to Six*, along with such titles as *Your Four Year Old: Wild and Wonderful* and *Your Six Year Old: Defiant but Loving*. Each contained detailed descriptions of what one might expect at each naturally unfolding age. Although the idea of readiness is no longer as popular as it once was, there are still educators and school systems that make use of the Gesell philosophy. The transitional kindergarten is one manifestation of the philosophy in action. The argument for it is that although everyone in a graduating kindergarten class may be close to 6 years old, it is likely that some children lack the mental maturity that will make it comfortable for them to learn to read. Because reading is the core of first-grade instruction, it would be better, the argument goes, to put the unready children into a class of their own. There, they can make the transition to first-grade learning at their own speed.

Letting children learn at their own speed while developing, flowerlike, in an expected sequence, is a Gesell idea that dates back to Rousseau. And whereas it may be argued that this vision of children is a limiting one, the strength of the philosophy—in these days of pushing children too far too soon—is its reluctance to do so.

Although many other historical figures have influenced early education, we complete our in-depth review by describing the two who have probably been the most important in recent times. In many ways they resemble each other, although their differences are often highlighted by educational writers. The first of these figures was a scientist devoted to genetic epistemology who actually preferred to leave the educational implications of his studies of children to other people.

Jean Piaget

Jean Piaget (1896–1980), like Rousseau and Pestalozzi before him, was born in Switzerland. And, like theirs, his childhood was a difficult one, if perhaps not as radically so. In writing about it many years later, he explained that his mother, although "intelligent, energetic, and fundamentally a very kind person," also had a "rather neurotic temperament" that "made our family life somewhat troublesome" (Piaget, 1953, p. 237). To shut off this difficult part of his life, Piaget chose at a very early age to follow an interest in science, modeling himself after his father, "a man of painstaking and critical mind, who dislikes hastily improvised generalizations. . . . Among other things he taught me the value of systematic work, even in small matters" (p. 237).

Turning aside childish play for serious study, Piaget published his first scientific observation (of an albino sparrow) when he was 10 years old. Later he apprenticed himself to a local natural history museum director and developed a lifelong interest in the study of mollusks. Although they were the subject of his doctoral dissertation, they were not the focus of any further study until the last few years of his life. Instead, Piaget took a position in Paris analyzing responses to items on standardized intelligence tests. Soon, he noticed that similar wrong answers were given by children of similar ages, and this led to interviews with the children to satisfy his curiosity as to why this was so. From this initial experience grew a lifelong dedication to the study of the genesis or origins of human knowledge: genetic epistemology.

He returned to Geneva, Switzerland, where he did research at the Institut Jean Jacques Rousseau, observing and interviewing children in the modified Montessori school there, marrying one of his graduate students, then publishing observations of his own children in their early years. Most of his observations of and interviews with children were devoted to cognitive development, but he also published one major study of children's moral development as well. Although his studies were published in the 1920s and 1930s, it was decades before they were translated into English and thus influential in the United States. Like Montessori, Piaget discovered that eager American educators wanted to use his ideas as a means to push children beyond their developmental readiness.

Piaget's ideas had elements in common with earlier philosophers and scientists, yet the way in which he fitted those elements into a new view was the work of a revolutionary genius. Piaget rejected the path of those who followed Rousseau in believing that children, like plants, simply needed good tending to grow to their genetically determined fullness. He also chose not to take the path begun by Locke in which children, with their blank slate minds, simply waited to be written on by a nurturing environment. Both nature and nurture, he said, affect how humans develop, so that we need not choose one path but must travel both. In Piaget's view, a child is born with certain genetic traits and, as he develops, interacts with the environment to construct his own intelligence. Piaget's view has been called *interactionism* or *constructivism*, the latter being the more popular term at this time.

To Piaget, there were four factors that explain early development: maturation, direct physical experience, social transmission, and equilibration. It is *equilibration* that is fundamental to school learning and refers to the child's continual process of cognitive self-correction, whose goal is a better sense of equilibrium. There are two subcategories of equilibration: *assimilation* and *accommodation*. When children learn something new that they can just add on to their existing store of logic (cognitive structure), they are said to assimilate it. For example, a baby who can crawl and who has seen a ball but never one that is rolling, can put these two bits of knowledge together to crawl after a ball the first time she sees one roll by her. Piaget said that assimilation has a close identification with play, thus making play important to adequate cognitive development.

Accommodation, on the other hand, might be termed more serious learning. In this case, some part of a child's cognitive structure has to be modified to take in the new learning. Suppose our crawling child has never seen a ball and suddenly one rolls by. The spherical shape, the rolling movement, perhaps the color are all new, and the child must adapt her thinking to take all this in. Of course, she may still take off after it, but the learning is deeper. As you might guess, both assimilation and accommodation go on continually and in combination with each other.

Despite his reluctance to give much advice to educators, Piaget did have some general ideas as to what should happen in the classroom. From the constructivist view, if children create their own intellects, then they should be given the freedom to do so. This argues for play, experimentation, and guided learning activities as opposed to direct instruction and lectures. As one example, Piaget abhorred the behaviorists' view of mathematics as a drill subject and argued instead for a rich variety of experiences that would lead to deeper understanding. Such learning should begin with concrete activities and only slowly give way to abstract experiences:

> Mathematical training should be prepared, starting at nursery school, by a series of exercises related to logic and numbers, lengths and surfaces, etc., and this type of concrete activity must be developed and enriched constantly in a very systematic way during the entire elementary education, to change little by little at the beginnings of secondary education into physical and elementary mechanical experiments. (Piaget, 1972, p. 104)

Piaget (1972) argued that it is better to let children spend more time on a few problems, really working through them, than to cover a lot of territory: "It is in learning to master the truth by oneself at the risk of losing a lot of time and of going through all the roundabout ways that are inherent in real activity" (p. 104). This approach to learning is more closely related to the current Japanese methods than it is to American ones, and every report of mathematical achievement indicates that what the Japanese are doing is more successful than the American concern with vast coverage of material.

Early critics of Piaget faulted him for basing his worldview of children on studies done in his own home. Subsequent research by others, however, seemed to indicate that his creative genius made it possible for him to do successfully what others would frown on. Today, early education is strongly influenced by Piaget, particularly when we put down the skillpacks and dittos in favor of less directive hands-on learning.

Lev Vygotsky

Our final historical figure is, like Piaget, of recent enough influence that research based on his ideas still goes on. If anything, his sphere of influence continues to grow, as Piaget's remains stable or even begins to diminish. Like Piaget, Lev Vygotsky

(1896–1934) can be understood and discussed as a constructivist, but his life experiences and political inclinations led him to different conclusions as to how constructions are made.

Probably the word most often used by biographers to describe Vygotsky's short and difficult life is tragic. Born into a Jewish family in czarist Russia, when an array of laws ensured that Jews could rarely rise to positions of influence or even live where they chose, the young Lev soon became known as a budding intellectual. His love for art, literature, history, and philosophy developed during his adolescence and continued to influence his ideas even years later when his academic interests became more focused on psychology and education (Berk & Winsler, 1995).

By the time Vygotsky was ready to enter university, the government had decreed that a lottery system would be used to determine which Jews would be chosen to fill the allotted 3% of the college population. Miraculously, Vygotsky's name was drawn, and he was permitted to enroll at Moscow University but not to study the fields he had come to love. Because these could only lead to a teaching career and Jews weren't allowed to teach, Vygotsky studied medicine for a while, then settled on law. Still restless to learn more, he coenrolled at Shaniavsky People's University, where professors who had left or been expelled from other institutions for their anticzarist stands had found a home. There, Vygotsky studied the subjects he had loved for so long and graduated from both universities in 1917.

As it turned out, 1917 was not only an important year for Vygotsky but for all of Russia, as anticzarist sentiment led to the government's downfall, revolutionary conflict and civil war, and the eventual creation of the Soviet Union with its foundations in Marxist socialism. Vygotsky, now able to teach the subjects he most cared about, did so, adding to them pedagogy as he became more and more committed to psychology and education.

In his mid-20s, Vygotsky joined a growing number of Russians who succumbed to tuberculosis, a disease from which he never fully recovered and which eventually cut short his remarkably productive life. During this same period he married, fathered two daughters, and impressed others sufficiently with his thoughts on psychology that he was invited to join the faculty of the Psychological Institute in Moscow.

As Vygotsky developed his theories of human development, he was influenced strongly by the political changes swirling about him. No fan of the repressive czarist regime, he adopted wholeheartedly the promising future that seemed to loom ahead in the Marxist Soviet Union. Thus, whereas Piaget, in the same years, envisioned a theory that dubbed children the creators of their own intelligence, Vygotsky focused on developing a more sociocultural or sociohistorical approach. In Piaget's case, the influences for his more individualistic view might be traced back to the renaissance of Greek and Roman thought and the rise of democracy; in Vygotsky's theory construction, the new social views pertaining to Marxism held sway.

For example, Vygotsky argued that children's development depended on social interaction and "participation in authentic cultural activities" as a mirror of history's development "by way of collective social movements and conflicts" (Berk & Winsler, 1995, p. 4). Vygotsky put so much emphasis on social interaction, in fact, that he believed it the most important element in the successful development of children with psychological or physical disabilities. That is, a child's underdevelopment of mental functions is less due to the disability itself than to "what we might call the isolation of an abnormal child from his collective." Applying this view to education, Vygotsky continued that whereas it would be "hopeless to battle with the defect and its natural consequences, it is valid, fruitful, and promising to struggle with difficulties in collective activities" (cited in Berk & Winsler, p. 83).

Vygotsky's views had a large influence on the thinking of his colleagues and students as well as on the larger psychological community as he took much of the leadership in his new country of reformulating "psychology according to Marxist methodology in order to develop concrete ways to deal with the massive tasks facing the Soviet Union" (Newman & Holzman, 1993, p. 6). It was, for Vygotsky and many others, a brief period of enthusiastic creativity and idealism.

In the 12 years following his first bout with tuberculosis, Vygotsky wrote or collaborated on nearly 200 papers, striving to complete his best known manuscript, *Thought and Language* (1934/1962), while on his deathbed. Despite this prodigious output, his work remained unknown outside his circle of colleagues and friends for many years. It was during these years that the dictator Joseph Stalin came to power, creating a repressive regime that squelched creativity and intellectual endeavors. This unfortunate period and beyond became the cold war years, in which little intellectual exchange between the United States and Soviet Russia took place. By the time *Thought and Language* was translated into English in 1962, Piagetian thought was uppermost in the minds of American educators and educational psychologists. It took another two decades before Vygotsky was truly discovered.

What Americans found when they discovered Vygotsky was a set of theoretical proposals that had been laid aside in some cases and, in others, expanded on over the decades by his colleagues. Some of Vygotsky's ideas complemented Piaget's, perhaps answering questions that Piaget's research had raised. Other ideas were more directly in conflict with Piaget's, based as they were on socialist ideals rather than on those of a more individualistic society. Some of the major Vygotskian ideas to know about are:

- *The importance of language to development.* Of all the symbol systems created by humans, language is the most important in Vygotsky's theory. In infancy, budding language capabilities are used for the sole purpose of social interaction; it is only later, in the preschool years, that language becomes a way of communicating with or influencing the behavior of the self. Because language is so important to early social development, and vice versa, Vygotsky had special concerns for deaf children. They would need extra coaching in their communication skills (primarily focused on lipreading in a time when sign language was not yet respected), and the intensity of the required training would lead to social isolation, a situation opposed to his general philosophy of effective development. Unfortunately, Vygotsky died before his views could be resolved and well before the prejudice against sign language was dispelled.

Both Piaget and Vygotsky observed preschool children talking to themselves, a phenomenon termed *private speech*. Piaget considered such behavior an example of the egocentric attempts at communication characteristic of the preoperational years, but Vygotsky viewed it as something quite different. Private speech, he observed, doesn't blossom into better communication during the concrete operational years but goes underground as children begin to whisper to themselves and eventually learn to carry on thought silently as adults do. Thus, he argued, private speech has nothing to do with communication with others and everything to do with communication with the self and even self-regulation of behavior.

Today researchers agree that there are times when preschoolers use language to communicate in egocentric ways, but they have come to prefer the Vygotskian view of private speech and base their studies on it rather than on Piaget's theory (Berk & Winsler, 1995). It should be noted that Piaget did not read Vygotsky's *Thought and Language* until it was translated from the Russian in the early 1960s. In the monograph he wrote in response to the book he stated, "I respect Vygotsky's position on the issue of egocentric speech, even though I cannot agree with him on all points" (Piaget, 1962).

• *Instruction leads and influences development.* Although Piaget agreed that education's role in child development was important, he also argued that teachers should avoid being too intrusive and intervene primarily for the purpose of facilitating the child's own self-construction. Vygotsky viewed the teacher—formal school teacher, parent, more knowledgeable peer, perhaps—as more directly important to development. His ideas were based, after all, on the importance of social interaction, and when applied to development, social interaction between teacher and learner would naturally hold importance.

The quality of such interaction would determine, to great extent, the quality of development, and the component of Vygotsky's theory we discuss next addresses this issue. Important to the quality of interaction is the teacher's ability to know when and to what extent to intercede in a child's learning and when to pull back. For example, a child who is quickly learning a concept or skill will generally benefit from little interaction with a teacher; a child with special learning needs may benefit most from specific, direct instruction extended over a longer period of time before independence is truly possible.

• *The zone of proximal development.* This zone is that space between what the child already knows or has mastered and the knowledge that is currently beyond his capabilities. It is the space where learning is challenging but not overly frustrating; where, with some help from a teacher, parent, or peer a child can develop new knowledge.

Vygotsky created the concept of the *zone of proximal development* (*ZPD*) in response to his own arguments against intelligence and other tests that determine what a child already knows and has accomplished. To explain his position, he used the analogy of a gardener who must test not only the mature fruit in his orchard but the developing fruit as well if he wishes to know how healthy the orchard really is. "If he is to fully evaluate the state of the child's development, the psychologist must consider not only the actual level of development but *the zone of proximal development*" (cited in Newman & Holzman, 1993, p. 56).

The concept of the ZPD is one that has been expanded by colleagues and researchers since Vygotsky's death. The next section is an example of just such expansion.

• *Scaffolding.* Vygotsky was certainly concerned about the teaching and learning that occurred within the ZPD, but it was for those who came after him to name and fully develop the idea of scaffolding. As in Piaget's theory of development, children are seen as self-builders. In Vygotsky's view, however, the role of the supportive social environment is of greater importance. The *scaffolding* provided by those in the child's social world helps him or her to develop to the fullest extent. It thus becomes a primary responsibility of the classroom teacher to identify, where possible, each child's ZPD and to provide just the right amount of guidance, direction, and encouragement to ensure optimum intellectual, social, and physical development.

Other Contributors

The people we have just discussed are arguably some of the most important figures in the history of early education, but there are many others who are worthy of our attention. Perhaps you have read about them, or soon will, in other contexts. Following is an annotated list of additional names you should know.

Socrates (470–399 B.C.): Greek philosopher and Plato's teacher who discussed the education of children under the age of 6.

Martin Luther (1483–1546): A German leader of the Protestant Reformation who introduced the idea of music as a school study. Luther believed girls should be educated, too.

Margarethe Schurz (1832–1876): Founded the first U.S. kindergarten in Watertown, Wisconsin, in 1855. Classes were conducted in German.

Elizabeth Peabody (1804–1894): Founded the first English-speaking U.S. kindergarten in Boston in 1860.

Susan Blow (1843–1916): Opened the first public kindergarten in the United States in 1873, with the backing and sponsorship of *William T. Harris*, superintendent of schools, St. Louis, Missouri.

Margaret McMillan (1860–1931): With the help of her sister *Rachel*, founded the first nursery school dedicated to improving the health and general well-being of preschool children in England. The building was in the style of a lean-to and open to the elements. The curriculum included both cognitive and social focuses.

Patty Smith Hill (1868–1946): A leader in the movement away from strict Froebelianism to more progressive education. She was influenced by Dewey as well as the psychologist *G. Stanley Hall*, both of whose philosophies were incompatible with much of Froebel's thought. At Teachers College, Columbia University, she cotaught a series of lectures with Susan Blow in which Hill's "common sense, practicality, and science" were pitted against Blow's "erudition, abstraction, and philosophy" (Shapiro, 1983, p. 167). From the point of view of most students and the administration, Hill came out the victor, and Froebelianism took one more step toward a natural death.

John B. Watson (1878–1958):   A psychologist who affected childrearing during the 1920s and 1930s. A behaviorist, he recommended little affection between parent and child, suggesting instead that children be treated as adults and given handshakes rather than hugs.

B. F. Skinner (1904–1990):   A behaviorist who believed that positive reinforcement is the impetus to increased learning. His thinking has influenced such school programs as assertive discipline, which makes extensive use of reinforcement. The use of extrinsic rewards for academic success is derived from behaviorist thought.

David Weikart: Founder of the Perry Preschool Project, which conducts research with disadvantaged children before and during the Head Start years. Follow-up studies have shown that the benefits of preschool are lasting, even into adulthood.

EXTENDING YOUR LEARNING

1. Choose one of the people listed in the last section and study his or her life and contributions to education. Share your findings with your class.

2. See if you can observe influences from centuries ago here in 21st-century America. Make a list of characteristics associated with education inspired by Locke and another list for Rousseau. Observe at least two classrooms, noting materials, teacher's style, children's learning behaviors and movement patterns, and teacher–child interaction. Compare your findings with the rest of your class.

3. Is there one best way to approach early education? Discuss the historical philosophies and theories and their most positive contributions. Would it be possible to combine the best of each to create the perfect early education? Why or why not?

4. Continue to reflect on your philosophy of early childhood education. Consider the positive and negative responses you had to the ideas of the various philosophers, psychologists, and educators. Some ideas for you to write down:

   • Choose one historic figure with whom you would like to study. What would you most like to learn?

   • Choose one historic figure with whom you would like to take issue. What are the major points you would like to make? What do you think this person might answer?

   • Select the ideas you like best and suggest ways you might be able to apply them in your own teaching life.

   • Select the ideas you like least and explain why you would be reluctant to use them with young children.

VOCABULARY

Accommodation. A cognitive process in which an internal mental structure is changed to incorporate new information.

Animism. The belief that inanimate objects make decisions about the ways in which they will act.

Assimilation. A cognitive process in which new information and experiences are incorporated into the existing internal mental structure.

Back to Basics. Educational emphasis on reading, writing, and arithmetic with little or no emphasis on the arts or other electives. Most recently given this name during the 1980s.

Casa dei Bambini. Italian for Children's House. The first school for young children established by Maria Montessori.

Cognitive. Pertaining to knowledge, information, and intellectual skills.

Concrete Operations. A Piagetian stage in which children are able to think about abstract concepts as long as they have concrete objects to manipulate or visualize.

Conservation. The understanding that materials or objects remain the same in weight or volume even though their shapes or arrangements in space may change.

Egocentric. In early infancy, being able to differentiate between what is and is not the self. Later, understanding the world only as it relates to the self.

Gifts and Occupations. Materials developed by Froebel for use with infants and young children.

Preoperational. The second Piagetian stage, from about age 2 to 7 or 8, in which children are able to use mental symbols and imagery; characterized by egocentric thinking linked to perception.

Private Speech. Speech that is not meant to communicate to anyone other than the speaker. It may be audible or not.

Self-correcting. Pertains to learning materials that have a control of user error built into the material itself.

Sensorimotor. The first Piagetian stage, from birth to about age 2, in which children learn about their environment through sensory input and physical actions.

Tabula Rasa. A blank slate; a term used by John Locke to represent the inexperienced mind of the child.

References

Berk, L., & Winsler, A. (1995). *Scaffolding children's learning: Vygotsky and early childhood education.* Washington, DC: National Association for the Education of Young Children.

Brosterman, N. (1997). *Inventing kindergarten.* New York: Abrams.

Cleverley, J., & Phillips, D. (1986). *Visions of childhood.* New York: Teachers College Press.

Comenius, J. A. (1896). *School of infancy.* Boston: Heath. (Original work published 1633)

Compayre, G. (1907). *Jean Jacques Rousseau and education from nature.* New York: Crowell.

deMause, L. (1974). *The history of childhood.* New York: Psychohistory Press.

Dewey, J. (1964). *John Dewey on education.* New York: Random House.

Elkind, D. (1983). *The hurried child.* Reading, MA: Addison-Wesley.

Gwynne-Thomas, E. H. (1981). *A concise history of education to 1900 A.D.* Washington, DC: University Press of America.

Kramer, R. (1976). *Maria Montessori.* Chicago: University of Chicago Press.

Locke, J. (1964). *John Locke on education.* New York: Teachers College Press.

Newman, F., & Holzman, L. (1993). *Lev Vygotsky: Revolutionary scientist.* New York: Routledge.

Osborn, D. K. (1980). *Early childhood education in historical perspective.* Athens, GA: Education Associates.

Pestalozzi, J. (1912). *Pestalozzi's educational writings.* London: Arnold.

Piaget, J. (1953). Autobiographie, Jean Piaget. In *A history of psychology in autobiography* (Vol. 4). Worcester, MA: Clark University Press.

Piaget, J. (1962). *Comments on Vygotsky's critical remarks concerning* The Thought and Language of the Child, *and* Judgment and Reasoning in the Child. Cambridge, MA: MIT Press.

Piaget, J. (1972a). *The principles of genetic epistemology.* New York: Basic Books.

Piaget, J. (1972b). *To understand is to invent.* New York: Viking Press.

Shapiro, M. (1983). *Child's garden.* University Park, PA: Penn State University Press.

Vygotsky, L. (1962). *Thought and language.* Cambridge, MA: MIT Press. (Original work published 1934)

Weber, E. (1984). *Ideas influencing early childhood education.* New York: Teachers College Press.

Wodehouse, H. (1924). *A survey of the history of education.* New York: Longmans, Green.

3

HOW THEORETICAL PERSPECTIVES SHAPE EARLY EDUCATION: SELECTED MODELS

The best school, after all, for the world of childhood, is not the school where children know the most answers, but the school where children ask the most questions.

Joe Coe

▼ Chapter Objectives

After reading this chapter, you should be able to:

▼ Describe, compare, and contrast six current models of early childhood education.

▼ Relate the six models to the theories and philosophies described in chapter 2.

As you think about and apply chapter content on your own, you should be able to:

▼ Begin to make your emerging philosophy of early education practical by developing a list of the kinds of places you can envision yourself happily working.

▼ Observe schools and centers with some understanding of their underlying theories and philosophies, whether overtly stated or not.

A glance around any selection of schools and centers for young children should inform the viewer that every site is not equal or the same. Without some explanation, however, it may be difficult to put one's finger on just what the differences are. There are schools that are directly influenced by theories or philosophies past or present, and the titles and mission statements of these schools make their identification obvious. As well, it is possible to visit schools and centers in which teachers are permitted to base educational practices on their personal philosophies, and parents can choose among them. Then, there are numerous child-care centers with no other guiding educational philosophy than the locally mandated standards for safety.

In this chapter, we visit six quite different schools and centers for young children. Their philosophies may differ widely, the youngsters vary in age from infants to children in primary grades, but in all cases the directors, caregivers, and teachers are committed to providing the best possible learning experiences. Where connections can be made to this book's first two chapters, this has been done, so that application of theory to the real world becomes apparent and job descriptions are seen in action.

Our first visit takes us to a complex of centers and activities all under the guiding concepts of the Head Start movement that began in the 1960s.

HEAD START: A UNIQUELY U.S. MODEL

The U.S. social and political turmoil and change of the 1960s were, in part, instigated by top-down political development. President John F. Kennedy's administration was committed to finding new ways of improving the economic status of the nation's poor, estimated at that time to be one fourth of the population. After Kennedy's death, President Lyndon Johnson enthusiastically took up the challenge, declaring a "war on poverty" whose goals were to both cure and prevent poverty in the United States.

As a first step, the Office of Economic Opportunity (OEO) was created in 1964, and a few months later Project Head Start was begun under its sponsorship. From the beginning, the focus of this program was to provide poor children of preschool age with some of the benefits middle-class society could more easily afford: day care, academic experiences, medical and dental care, and involvement at many levels for the parents. Originally planned as a pilot program for 100,000 children in the summer of 1965, the national clamor to be part of this unique creation led to an initial enrollment of more than 550,000 children in over 11,000 centers. For the next few years, Head Start grew in size and popularity, while also extending the summer program to a full year at most sites. Then the first national review of its effectiveness was published.

In 1969, the Westinghouse Learning Corporation was commissioned to evaluate the impact on school achievement of children who were graduates of the program. The results were dismaying. Although the children's cognitive and affective gains were positive during their time in Head Start, any growth flattened out and diminished during the primary years. By this time, Richard Nixon was president, and his initial enthusiasm for the program quickly abated, as did congressional funding (Washington & Oyemade, 1987).

Over the next several years, Head Start fought for its existence. As a beginning, the OEO published a review of all Project Head Start research, demonstrating that the program was more successful than the Westinghouse study indicated (Kirschner Associates, 1970). Yet, many thought Head Start had died, particularly after it was reported to have done so in some major newspapers (Washington & Oyemade Bailey, 1995). Congressional support varied and waivered over the years until the first longitudinal studies showed what happened to Head Start children as they moved toward and into adulthood. The most widely reported study was one that followed 123 children from the Perry Preschool in Yspilanti, Michigan, into their 27th year (Schweinhart & Weikart, 1993). The researchers found that in their adulthood, the preschool graduates were more likely than their peers who had never attended preschool to own homes, complete higher levels of education, require fewer social services, and be in less trouble with the law.

In recent years, such reports of success have gone a long way to promote public and congressional awareness of and support for Head Start and its several programs. Always a work in progress, Head Start has continually experimented with a variety of programs to meet differing needs while being moved from one government agency to another (it is currently housed in the U.S. Department of Health and Human Services.) By the late 1990s, more than 800,000 children between the ages of 3 and 5 were enrolled in more than 37,000 Head Start classrooms. Children with disabilities accounted for 13 percent of the total.

Although the original model for preschoolers is the most widely known and commonly found, other programs have evolved over the years as well. Some, but by no means all, of Head Start's innovations, national demonstration models, and strategies include:

• *Early Head Start.* Established in 1994 as research was showing the critical importance of healthy development in the first 3 years of life. The purpose of Early Head Start is to foster the cognitive, social and emotional, and physical growth of newborns to 3-year-olds while helping parents to be better teachers and caregivers of their infants and toddlers. Included too is help for parents in meeting their own life goals, including financial independence. In this program, education can take place either in the home or at a Head Start center; help for parents can be provided on an individual basis, through peer support groups, or both.

• *Home Start.* Provides home-based educational, health, and social services, primarily in rural areas. The Head Start teacher works with both the at-home parent and child(ren). In some cases, children may participate in Home Start while they are 3 years old, then attend a Head Start preschool the following year.

• *Even Start.* Unites early childhood education (through age 7) and adult basic education. While their children attend a Head Start center or elementary school, parents are provided with help in literacy acquisition, vocational training, or study for the GED (general equivalency diploma), for instance. Parenting education is an integral part of the program with goals that include building stronger family networks and improving parent and child self-esteem.

• *Child Development Associate (CDA).* This national credentialing program, once part of the Head Start framework, is now operated by the Council for Early Childhood Professional Recognition in Washington, DC. More than 90 percent of Head Start's teachers have teaching certification, and most of these hold the CDA. The credential can be earned through a combination of on-site mentoring and coursework, often through a local community college. The core curriculum is determined by the four focii of the Head Start program: education, health, parent involvement, and social services.

To see some Head Start initiatives in action, we will visit a rural area in northwest Washington State, close to the Canadian border.

Head Start Preschool and Much More, All Under One Local Umbrella

It is unusual to see such a large variety of Head Start-related resources in one rural community, but strong leadership and community cooperation have led to an increasing number of family services. In addition to the services described here, also emerging is an alternative high school complete with child care.

The Head Start Program

We will begin our several visits at the Head Start center. In general, when people think of the national program, a setting such as this for 4- and 5-year-olds is what they envision. Like many centers, the Nooksack Head Start is located in a homelike building next to a public school, in this case the local high school. In a large room that serves about 20 children, Michael Marsh and Julie Emerson[1] share teaching responsibilities with the help of a classroom aide. Several of the children are just learning English and whereas Michael can speak Spanish to those who come from Mexico, children who have immigrated from Ukraine, Russia, Vietnam, and the Punjab must use other clues to understand what is going on.

It is 9:30 A.M. when we begin our visit, the time that the children are divided into two groups of 10 for special projects and snack with their assigned teacher. Michael divides his group of children further, for a choice of planting popcorn seeds or an art project, but Julie's group works together on a counting lesson involving fish-shaped crackers that are eaten by her 10 "hungry sharks." It is about 10:00 A.M. when both groups finish their activities and begin to prepare for snack.

Head Start academic curricula and teaching styles can vary considerably in different sites across the United States, but snack and meal times share a focus on nutrition, community building, traditional family serving styles, and growth in good manners. To see how this works, let's observe Julie and her group during the 30 minutes it takes to complete the entire experience.

A kitchen helper has wheeled in a large serving cart with small bagels already placed on plastic plates and applesauce served up in small bowls. With everyone seat-

---

[1]All children's names have been changed; teachers' names have not.

ed at a single rectangular table, their hands freshly washed, Julie demonstrates how each plate and bowl should be passed in one direction. She then carefully helps herself to some cream cheese, shows how it should be placed on the plate, then passed around the table. Spreading the cheese on the bagel, Julie points out that it is important to spread after passing so that people don't have to wait so long for their food. Finally, a pitcher of milk is also passed, with Julie demonstrating proper pouring techniques. When a bit is spilled by one child, she assures him that "It's okay—this happens sometimes" and helps him wipe up the spill.

When all the food has been distributed, Julie reminds the children that she always likes to wait until everybody has their food before she begins eating. This comment, and those that have preceded it, are not news to the children but rather are daily reminders of proper behavior. When Julie makes this final suggestion, not a single child has begun eating.

For the next few minutes, as everyone eats, Julie engages the children in polite conversation, asking what they have enjoyed doing during the extended weekend that has just passed. When the children are finished, they clear their own places, putting spoons and knives to soak in soapy water and plastic dishes in the trash. Circle time and free-choice centers round out the half-day program.

The curricular framework for this Head Start center was developed cooperatively with a local expert in early childhood education. It is based, for the most part, on the positions taken by the National Association for the Education of Young Children (NAEYC) regarding developmentally appropriate practices. In addition, each child has an individual learning plan (ILP) developed cooperatively with his or her parents. Because there are many varieties of curriculum and teaching methodologies found in Head Start centers, visits to one or more nearby sites are recommended for our readers.

The Home Start Program

Heidi Bugby's time is split between the Nooksack Head Start center and her visits to the homes of 3-year-old children who are scheduled to begin the Head Start program when they turn 4. She meets each of her 10 children once a week in their homes, then works with them again on Thursdays when they all join the 4-year-olds at the center.

Each home visit is 2 hours long and is divided into three typical Head Start components: social services, parenting and child development, and one-on-one educational work with the child. Heidi enters each home with planned topics for discussion with the parent and activities for the child, but she remains flexible. On the day of our visit, she spends more than her usual time with the parent, although there is still plenty of time left for a major activity with the child, as we shall see.

Alexei, his older sister, and parents live in a mobile-home park located in a wooded area at the foot of a mountain range. This is an area populated to great extent by immigrants from the former Soviet Union; Alexei's family immigrated from Ukraine 8 years ago. Although his father has been able to find well-paying work, his mother, Ivana, has not. In addition, Alexei, who speaks almost no English, will begin school

Head Start programs are not only for children. Their parents also have opportunities for learning.

at the Head Start center in a few months. At his last weekly visit with the other 3-year-olds, he engaged in some misbehavior that Heidi had trouble redirecting because of the linguistic barrier between them. These issues will guide today's visit as each of the Head Start components is met.

A small but comfortable dining room serves as Heidi's classroom, and she begins by discussing with Ivana a combination of information about upcoming Head Start activities and progress on finding a job appropriate to Ivana's training, work background, and bilingual capabilities. Heidi has brought a letter she has written as reference and discusses Ivana's resumé, which they are working on together. Conversation then moves to Alexei's behavior the previous week, and Heidi suggests one or two ways that Ivana might talk to Alexei about it "without making him feel bad." The discussion of Head Start activities, job hunts, and Alexei's behavior takes just over an hour and combines, in a friendly and informal way, the first three components of the Head Start program (social services, parenting and child development, educational work with the child).

During this discussion, Alexei has been happily involved in creating ever more complex structures from a set of snap-blocks brought by Heidi. For the most part, he has played by himself, though occasionally he walks shyly around Heidi and whispers to his mother, usually to share a description of what he has just made.

During the second hour, Heidi, Ivana, and Alexei all participate in the making of a piñata, a craft activity designed to allow informal conversation in English and to help varying cultures represented at the center learn more about each other. As they work, Heidi practices learning various colors in their language while Alexei learns them in English. It is an important aspect of Head Start that immigrant children learn English and U.S. cultural values but that they also do not lose their original language and culture. Thus, Heidi shows her respect for what she sees in this Ukrainian immigrant home while preparing Alexei for the experiences he will have in the culture of the United States.

As we leave, Heidi admires the pots of flowers Ivana has planted near the front door, reminds Alexei that she will see him Thursday and that he should wear something green (*ziloni*) because it is the color of the week.

The Even Start Program

Across the street from the center, in an out-of-the-way wing of the high school, a comfortable classroom and adjacent office space have been assigned to the local Even Start program. Here, parents whose reading skills are less than those of an eighth grader and who lack high school diplomas, gather several times a week for an array of educational services. Parent education is provided by a nearby technical college. Adult basic education comes from the county's community college. Much or most of the curriculum is individualized, since each parent comes in with his or her own educational accomplishments and goals. (Currently, all the parents are mothers.)

In addition to the on-campus education, there are home visits provided if the family has a child in Head Start. Public health nurses, social workers, and bilingual educators all provide services as needed.

The success of this program can be seen in parental comments such as these:

"I never thought I'd get a second chance to go back . . . and here I am, 6 months into my high school diploma! I'm watching my kids grow and they're watching me, too!"

"I wasn't doing anything . . . just sitting at home and watching TV. Now, I spend time reading to my kids and I'm almost done with my GED!"

The Infant–Toddler Program

While their mothers attend Even Start classes, those children too young to attend Head Start are provided with care in a light and open portable classroom on the school grounds. Just as the other programs we described focus on enhancing each individual's learning, so too does this program. It emphasizes providing the children with stablity, predictability, and consistency through scheduled naps, meals, and other healthful routines. The staff also works to create a safe environment in which nothing is off-limits to beginning explorers.

Once each week, parents join their children at the care center for a special Parent and Child Together (PACT) session. Here, the skills learned in the parenting classes can be discussed and put into practice with support from peers and instructors.

All the programs described here grew from the federally funded Project Head Start, but they also receive funding and other support from local agencies and schools. There is a strong emphasis on collaboration and cooperation along with a continual assessment of every program so that improvements can be made and new ideas instituted. As mentioned earlier, Head Start has always been a work in progress.

In our next section, we look at another approach to early education and care that can take a number of forms. In this case, however, national support is sporadic and even more tied to political history. In a nation that values capitalism and remains conflicted about how much government should be involved in the welfare of families and their young children, this is, perhaps, inevitable. The ways that corporations handle employees who have young children vary widely.

CORPORATE CHILD CARE IN THE UNITED STATES

Although child care has always been an issue for working mothers and single parents, it was the beginning of the 1970s when a corporation provided its own center for the children of workers. The Stride Rite shoe company in Massachusetts opened its doors to the children of employees and outsiders as well, then pioneered once again when in 1990 it invited elders needing care to join them. In the intervening years, more than 8,000 employer-supported centers have opened around the United States, and the number continues to grow as more and more corporations and government agencies, such as the military, discover that the benefits far outweigh the costs (Seitel, 1998).

For example, Stride Rite has calculated that providing child care creates a corporate saving of $22,000 per employee due to the ability to retain valuable personnel and avoid training replacements. Many other companies also report an increased retention rate once child care is provided. Morale improves too, even among those employees who have no children. A hospital in Minnesota, for example, found that a parent worried about lack of child care could be a burden to coworkers, a situation that resolved itself once on-site care was provided. At the same hospital, administrators report that employees who consider leaving have been known to stay because they don't want to remove their children from the center. Furthermore, the same center has been a magnet for desirable job applicants (Seitel, 1998).

Many companies, particularly smaller ones, may provide assistance to employees other than on site. They may work informally, for example, with a small selection of existing centers or even private homes in the neighborhood. Other companies provide backup or emergency care in an on-site center. Chase Manhattan Bank, for instance, not only provides emergency care but has become the first corporation to have such a center accredited by NAEYC.

Despite continued positive reports from corporations large and small since the 1970s, child care continues to be a problem for many working families. In 1989, with the intent of identifying and addressing "the pressing questions around how to create stronger families, more supportive communities, and more effective workplaces" including such issues as child care, the Families and Work Institute was established, with funding supplied by foundations and corporations (Families and Work Institute,

1998, p. 9). The institute participates in research projects, publications, and conferences. A major theme of its 1999 Work and Family Conference was "What's new in child care, elder care, working with supervisors, and culture change?" It is apparent that by the end of the century, elder care had become an issue for discussion, just as child care has been for many decades.

In the 1990s, child care became part of the national political discussion at the same time that concern for the disintegration of families became a national preoccupation. The Clinton White House began sponsoring a series of "Family Re-Unions" in 1991, each with its own theme. By 1996, the fifth Re-Union was designed to focus on family relationships and work experiences. A major issue for discussion was the continuing problem of child care for working families, with a focus on the provision of high-quality care that can foster in children the best social, emotional, and psychological development (Family Re-Union V, 1996).

The following year, a White House Conference on Child Care took place not long after widely reported research was published showing the importance of the early years to lifelong development. Yet as President Clinton noted at that time, the 1995 Census showed that families were having to pay as much as 25% of their income on child care (Clinton, 1997).

As corporations continue to step in to meet their employees' needs, a number of models of care and education emerge. The one described here may be fairly typical of what one might see in centers across the United States.

Early Education and Care as Provided by St. Joseph's Hospital in Washington State

St. Joseph's Hospital's stated mission includes service to the local community, and its child-care centers are included in that outreach. The centers were established primarily as a convenience to hospital employees, but anyone may choose to enroll their children, and many do.

The hospital is located at two campuses on opposite sides of town, with the child-care centers in a residential area that abuts the south campus. It is a neighborhood of older, often Victorian-style, homes of modest size. Two houses across the alley from the hospital provide one center for toddlers and another for preschoolers. The two are surrounded by a single fence and connected by a gravel-covered play area, complete with a shed for storage and rainy day play. In addition, there is a "sick bay" in the hospital for children from infancy through 11 years old who have noncontagious illnesses. These may be children belonging to hospital employees, from the child-care center, or from the child-care centers at two local colleges.

Overseeing all three centers is a manager of children's services rather than a director, although her responsibilities are similar to those in a more traditional child-care center. In addition to having the sick bay, however, there are a few other differences between this and the more traditional center. Because Children's Services is considered an integral part of the hospital, its employees clean and sanitize the centers nightly and provide all maintenance and repair free of charge to the center. And,

Although corporate child care may be provided as a baby sitting service for working parents, high quality centers also provide experiences for learning.

although the public is welcome to use all facilities, hospital employees pay less than outsiders, both at the centers and the sick bay.

Inside the two centers, an observer can see what might be termed a traditional U.S. approach to early education. The hospital and center staff refer to their mission as primarily one of child care, but there is still much attention given to curriculum. Thus, in both houses there are scheduled story and music sessions, circle times, and games that stress various types of learning. Each month, parents receive a calendar that provides an overview of upcoming curriculum that is designed to encourage development in each of five areas: social, emotional, intellectual, physical, and creative.

Despite the staff's focus on optimum development, typically just one or two children are enrolled for educational purposes only. Most of the 8 to 10 toddlers and 12 to 15 preschoolers attend because their parents were looking for quality child care. Many or most of these parents are aware that St. Joseph's is one of only two child-care centers in the area that have been certified by NAEYC.

Such certification entails an entire year of self-study by the staff on issues as diverse as multiculturalism, physical safety, and the developmental appropriateness of the curriculum. As a part of the study, parents are surveyed extensively, and a representative of NAEYC goes on site to validate the findings of the self-study. A modified self-study every subsequent 3 years leads to certificate renewal. This NAEYC certifying program holds a national reputation as an indicator of quality child care and education. Centers typically undergo the intensive application process when their staff and environment are of sufficient quality that the requirements are well under-stood and accepted. For a corporate-sponsored center with a community mission such as St. Joseph's, the NAEYC certificate identifies the center as a leader in the community and a showcase of quality.

MONTESSORI'S INFLUENCE ON U.S. EARLY EDUCATION

Working parents' need for child care has been with us since the advent of the indus-trial revolution. It has been almost a century since the owners of slum apartments in Rome contracted with Maria Montessori to provide a day-care center for the children who played unsupervised while their parents were at work. The owners' interests were less with the children than with the survival of their buildings. Happily for the children, Montessori's interests were with them. Here is the story of the schools that grew from that experience.

Chapter 2 presented an overview of the life and ideas of Maria Montessori, Italy's first female medical doctor and influential leader in the development of 20th-centu-ry early childhood education. Because of her continuing influence almost one-half century after her death, we include here a more in-depth description of the schools that bear her name.

The social environment of a Montessori class, as you will recall from chapter 2, is designed to foster in children independence, cooperation, sharing, responsibili-ty, even grace and courtesy—all qualities necessary for the creation of a predemo-cratic *society in embryo*, as Montessori called it. Montessori believed that it was unnecessary, even futile, to attempt to goad young children into developing these qualities through intrusive adult teaching methods, and so the teachers in her schools rely on a carefully crafted environment instead. The focus is on letting chil-dren develop as individuals, and as they do, they come naturally into the beginnings of a successful society. Materials and furniture are designed and arranged in such a way that children can choose whether to work independently or with others; the teacher intervenes in a child's decisions only if a continuing problem arises. Gen-erally, there are few materials found in multiples. Instead, a single sample of each type is available, thus making it necessary for children to take turns and share. The teacher's responsibility is to work with the children to design an equitable system, thus providing them with an opportunity to develop as individuals and create their embryonic society.

The social structure is also enhanced by the mixing of ages. This provides children with an experience more representative of real life than a single-age class would. More specifically, the younger children learn to rely on the older ones for assistance while the older children experience responsibility and caring.

The academic environment of a Montessori school is a bit different—at times it can be profoundly different—from that in most other preschools. The social structure just described plays an important part in academic learning. For example, more knowledgeable children take an active part in teaching what they know to their class-mates. At the same time, young children are more likely to work on their own than they are in most preschools or centers. Montessori observed that there was a *sensitive* or *critical period* at the younger ages for self-development best fostered, she believed, by not forcing group work and play.

Academic materials in a Montessori preschool tend to be quite structured with very specific purposes. Whereas there is certainly room for creativity, the Montessori philosophy is that creativity grows best from the experience of reality. Thus, when a new skill or learning is encountered, children are provided with self-correcting materials and direct instruction. Later, exploration and creativity are permitted. Even at this more advanced stage, however, there may be limits. For example, a series of 10 wooden (usually pink) cubes that increase in size from 1 to 100 square centimeters may be built into a vertical tower, a horizontal tower, or even combined with other similar materials to make intricate patterns. The cubes, however, may not be turned into a choo-choo train or a doll house but must always keep their original academic intent.

The role of the teacher in a Montessori school is considered that of guide, director, or facilitator. It is with the purpose of serving the children's needs and interests that the teacher steps back when possible in order to observe their behaviors and to allow the embryonic society to develop. In all ways, teachers model appropriate behaviors: carrying chairs and materials carefully, taking care not to bump into children's work and helping to fix things if they do, speaking and moving with a sense of quietness.

In the following description of a Montessori school, you see examples of these elements in action. In addition, two different classrooms within the school are described so that connections between what children learn at a young age and carry forward over the years can be seen.

The Montessori Approach at the Aidan Montessori School in Washington, DC

Originally founded as the St. Aidan School by Roman Catholic parents, the school has now been secularized and moved to a central location so that it might serve all the city. The ethnic diversity of the children as well as of the teaching staff reflects the success of this venture. There are four age levels represented in the multiage classes: 18 months to 3 years, 3 to 6 years, 6 to 9 years, and 9 to 12 years. Our visit takes us to two of these classrooms on the second day of a new school year.

Denise Merkel, teacher of the toddler class, considers the development of independence an issue from the first day of school and provides the children with careful instructions for such skills as washing their own hands, using the toilet, and taking coats on and off. Beginning socialization skills include choosing their own work, waiting turns, pushing chairs in carefully, and becoming more graceful in their movements throughout the room. Denise introduces all of these skills by demonstration and modeling, then providing encouragement to the children as they endeavor to repeat what she does.

Montessori classrooms are designed so that children can choose to work either in groups or independently.

Most of the eight children in her class are returnees and have some familiarity with the expected behaviors and routines. Still, one of the 2½-year-olds suddenly becomes homesick on this, her second day of the new year. Denise goes to her and a few of the others crowd around as well. "I want my daddy to pick me up," Annie cries. Soon, Denise has all the children telling the group who will be picking them up and Annie becomes calm.

During the discussion, Edward is at the other end of the room spooning hazelnuts from one bowl into another, a *practical life* exercise designed to help the youngest children learn to participate skillfully in everyday life. Occasionally he contributes a comment to the discussion with Annie and finally goes to join the group. Gently, Denise tells him, "You need to finish your work. Go finish your spooning." He returns to his little table with its single chair and spoons the nuts for another minute or 2, finally returning the materials to their proper place on the open-shelving system. Denise notices, however, that Edward has left his chair out, and she sends him back to replace it correctly. She does this without any trace of criticism in her voice and Edward accepts the correction with equanimity, pushing the chair in as well as a 2-year-old can, then joins a group beginning to collect around the guinea pig's cage.

For the next half-hour, the children wander the room, sometimes deciding on materials to work on alone or with others, sometimes following the teacher as she shows a child a table-washing activity and demonstrates to others how to water a plant. At one point, Annie asks, "Is Daddy here yet?" but seems undisturbed to be told he isn't. Forty minutes into their 2-hour day, the entire group settles happily into self-chosen activities, occasionally exchanging them for others after correctly returning the originals to their proper places.

Meanwhile, the primary class (3- to 6-year-olds) is also adjusting to its first week of school. All the children are returnees, with new children scheduled to begin a few days later, after the rhythm of the class has been established. The teacher, Kajal Guha, displays much the same behavior as Denise does in the toddler class, roving quietly through the room looking for opportunities to teach and lend support. In both classes, this roving is not casual and unplanned. The teachers have ideas in advance about the children they plan to work with and the materials they will introduce.

In this, the middle of the second morning of the first week of school, Kajal is most concerned with the social processes that must be established early on if learning is to flow smoothly the rest of the year. Like Denise, she keeps an eye out for the social processes that would benefit from some practice.

As she observes and interacts with children working, sometimes alone and sometimes in pairs, on such activities as puzzle maps, easel painting, and table scrubbing, Kajal notes that one clean-up routine is not being accomplished easily by several children. Since many of the children work on the floor in a Montessori classroom, they are provided with small rugs that are kept rolled up in a storage bin when not in use. The children in Kajal's class have had much practice in unrolling and rerolling the rugs, but after the summer vacation, several have lost their earlier expert touch, and the rugs are beginning to flop chaotically from their bin.

Kajal decides that a reminder demonstration of rug-rolling techniques would be useful for the entire group of 12 children. She gathers them around her on the large oriental rug that is used at group time, with the children using the exterior border as a guide for sitting. Three children, however, have not finished the work they started on the far side of the room and show no interest in joining the larger group. Kajal determines that it is more important just now for these three to experience the satisfaction that comes with completion of an activity than to join the goup in an activity that can be repeated later, so she makes no suggestions to them about hurrying to join the class or interrupting their work for the demonstration.

The nine remaining children watch as Kajal shows them how to roll the rug. She makes no comments about the fact that they have known this before and seem to have lost their expertise; all is done without criticism or even coaxing children to improve. Then, the children take turns rolling several mats with the teacher encouraging their effort and complimenting their skill. At the other end of the room, the classroom aide helps the remaining three children finish their work and, eventually, they join the others in rug rolling.

Suddenly, Georg shouts a question to the aide, shattering the serenity of the moment. Everyone except the teacher looks a bit startled. Kajal simply asks quietly, "Can anyone tell us why we don't shout?"

Children raise their hands and answer, "It bothers the other classes," or "We can't work," or "It's rude," and "It can get annoying."

"What do we do instead?" Kajal asks.

"We walk to the other teacher," someone answers, and Georg walks to the other end of the room and talks quietly to the aide.

Translating Philosophy to Different Settings

If we look closely at the two classrooms in this very typical Montessori school, we see different teaching approaches that reflect the different ages of the children. We also see close connections and careful transitions between the ages. Both Denise and Kajal take time at the beginning of the year to establish routines that show respect for the materials as well as one another and contribute to the smooth functioning of the classroom. In addition, there are underlying values of personal independence coupled with the creation of a predemocratic group ethic—Montessori's society in embryo. For example, when Denise and Kajal carefully teach a specific method for rolling a rug or placing a chair at its table, their intent is to help the children achieve independence and competence while learning that what they do is a courtesy to the children who wish to use the materials next. Such simple activities, multiplied over time and among children, lead to a cohesive group that is, nevertheless, made up of very independent individuals.

The Aidan Montessori School was chosen for its excellence in demonstrating Montessori's ideas, but one could visit almost any other Montessori school and recognize the philosophy in action, even though historically there have been schisms among various groups, all of which purport to teach the "real" Montessori curriculum. There is, for example, a core collection of manufactured materials, all of them containing some form of self-correction. All the manufactured materials as well as those made by the teachers are placed on child-height shelving with divisions made according to categories (for example, math, language, practical life, and materials for learning through the various senses.) The observer of this environment in action would see children making their own choices of work; deciding whether they wish to work alone or with others; and, for that matter, a focus on *work* as opposed to *play*, although this terminology is more for the purpose of showing respect for the children's activities than it is for taking away their enjoyment. The children would seem, to most observers, to be quite content with their school lives.

EDUCATING THE WHOLE CHILD: THE AESTHETIC PERSPECTIVE OF WALDORF SCHOOLS

Our next model of early education is, no doubt, the most unusual one we will study. It is also the one that is least likely to be adopted by public or more traditional schools, although in some respects, it has influenced education in ways both subtle and global. For this reason, we now look at the history of Waldorf schools and view an example in British Columbia, Canada.

The unusual nature of Waldorf education has been described by one writer (Kotzsch, n.d.) as "like passing through Alice's looking glass into an educational wonderland. It is a surprising, sometimes disorienting world of fairy tales, myths and legends, of music, art, physics demonstrations, class plays and seasonal festivals, of workbooks written and illustrated by students, a world without exams, grades, computers or televisions. It is, in short, a world where most of the standard ideas and practices of American education have been stood on their heads" (p. 2).

The history of this approach to education began in a most unlikely place, a German cigarette factory. In April 1919, just a few months after the end of World War I, a philosopher named Rudolf Steiner (1861–1925) gave a talk about politics, economics, and education to a gathering of workers at the Waldorf-Astoria cigarette factory in Stuttgart, Germany. It was Steiner's view that people such as the Waldorf workers and their children should not be subjected to an education that simply trained them for an industrial society. Rather, they should have an education that developed their natural talents and permitted their individual personalities to bloom.

The owner of the factory was so impressed with Steiner's talk that he immediately asked him to begin a school for the workers. Steiner agreed to do so as long as children of all social and economic backgrounds could attend, the curriculum would cover an entire 12 years, and its religious orientation would be nondenominational. His conditions were agreed to, and by fall of the same year, the Waldorf School had opened (Uhrmacher, 1995).

During the next few years, similar schools were founded in Germany, the Netherlands, and Great Britain. In 1928, the first Waldorf school opened in the United States, in New York City. By the end of the 20th century, more than 500 schools could be found worldwide, with more than 200 of them in North America.

The influences on Steiner's philosophy and views of education were several and included both Western and Eastern thought. Putting them together, he created a new philosophy that he named *anthroposophy* (from *anthropos* or man and *sophia* or wisdom.) A key tenet of anthroposophy is that even the most ordinary human being is capable of becoming more spiritual. The activities he suggested for achieving a spiritual state include several that had immediate application for education from the earliest ages: "cultivating one's sense of the beautiful, sympathizing with fellow beings, thinking . . . and developing powers of observation" (Uhrmacher, 1995, p. 387).

Anthroposophy defines human development as a journey of the soul from birth to death to rebirth through reincarnation, but it is the stages of child development Steiner posited that are reflected in a Waldorf school. In some ways, the Steiner stages are similar to those Piaget theorized in that their divisions appear at about the same chronological time and their cognitive elements have implications for classroom teaching (Ginsburg, 1982). Piaget's views, however, are those of the scientist whereas Steiner's come from a philosophical orientation. To Steiner, the development of cognition was only part of an educator's focus; the journey of soul and spirit was equally important, if not more so.

Steiner viewed the first stage of child development, birth to age 7, as a time of imitation, of learning through empathy and by doing. Thus, it becomes important for influential adults to model only the behavior they wish to see imitated. Everything from tone of voice to "physical touch, bodily gesture, light, darkness, color, harmony and disharmony" are influences that "are absorbed by the still-malleable physical organism and affect the body for a lifetime" (Barnes, 1991, p. 52). Education for this age, according to Steiner, should not push children into academic pursuits. Reading instruction, which could actually cause more harm than good if provided too early, should wait while more important activities are engaged in. These include various art activities, in which imitation of the teacher does not carry the negative stigma it does in other models of early education; story time, in which the teacher creates and tells stories appropriate to a particular class, so that children can imagine the pictures for themselves; and *eurythmy*, an art form created by Steiner that involves movement, rhythm, language, and music.

Middle childhood begins, in Steiner's philosophy, about the time children's baby teeth are lost and the *etheric life force*, or vital energy that differentiates living beings from minerals, emerges, somewhere around age 6. Whereas the first stage is characterized by imitation, this second stage focuses on feeling and rhythm. As children learn their arithmetic tables, they chant them rhythmically or sing songs to help them memorize. Eurythmy is continued from the earlier years, as is story telling. The latter is focused on fairy tales in the first grade, fables in the second, and Old Testament stories in the third—all with the idea that these forms of literature appeal to the feeling mode of children in the second stage of development.

One major component of Waldorf education for all ages is the 2-hour block of study at the beginning of each day. This was originated to counteract the fragmentation of the curriculum in early 20th-century Germany, but Waldorf educators could just as easily point to the same problem in American education today.

Another component is the division of faculty into *class* and *specialty* teachers. The class teacher stays with a single group of children from first through eighth grade, providing continuity while also being mindful of the children's changing needs and interests. Specialty teachers are experts in particular areas such as eurythmics or art. In the early grades, the teacher is viewed less as a facilitator than as the classroom leader—not in an authoritarian way, but as one who is definitely in charge of what learning goes on. There is sensitivity to children's interests, but it is the teacher, not children or administrators, who determine the curriculum.

Third, classroom environment and tools of learning are created with an eye focused closely on the aesthetic. This is probably to be expected in an approach to education that focuses on arts and crafts more than any other model does. Natural materials are used where possible. Thus, walls are painted with careful attention to both color and texture, fabrics are often hand dyed, and beeswax is prized as the best material for crayons and one of the most aesthetic substances for modeling projects. Few commercial textbooks are used, technology is reserved for later years, and teachers, often with the children's help, create most learning materials.

Finally, although anthroposophic philosophy guides curriculum and teaching methodology, Waldorf schools do not intend to create new generations of anthroposophists. Children are not in any way indoctrinated; indeed, they may attend their school for years and never hear the words *anthroposophy* or *Steiner* (Kotzsch, n.d.).

Putting all these elements together into a unified whole creates a school setting that is at once similar to and different from any others we might observe. To see Steiner's philosophies in practice, we go now to North Vancouver, British Columbia.

Aesthetics in Practice at the Vancouver Waldorf School

It is 9:00 A.M. and Pat Tatum's 25 third graders sit in rows of two-person desks, facing the blackboard in front and practicing songs on their recorders. At first, the scene appears much like that of any traditional third-grade class led by their teacher in a direct instruction lesson. Then, subtle differences become noticeable. The children sit in beautifully crafted wooden chairs. The contours of the room form an indefinable geometric shape with corners in unexpected places. The walls are painted in restful pastel shades. And on the chalkboard is a large, teacher-drawn picture of a *sukkah*, an integral part of the Hebrew Sukkot holiday the children have been studying. Next to the picture is a story the teacher has written in a beautiful cursive hand, words alternating in three colors of chalk. The story tells of the children's experiences in making their own version of a sukkah:

> In honor of the harvest we made a little house. It had three walls. We made a roof by nailing boards across the top. We put branches on top also. When people climbed on it our shelter fell down.

At this moment, however, story and picture await the appropriate time for the class's attention. The focus is on memorizing the recorder music and, eventually, on singing.

When it is time to move on to the morning's arithmetic lesson, the class does so, quite literally. Pat clasps two large wooden sticks in her hands, beating them and chanting in rhythm, "Move those chairs. Work those muscles." The children know just what to do, and soon everything has been replaced close to the walls leaving a large space for very active learning. After a couple full-group songs that place everyone in a large circle, subcircles are formed with each one in turn playing a chanting game that includes the multiplication tables they are currently studying. Next, children return to the larger circle where they divide into pairs to chant and clap the same tables. This time, however, they also work backward, starting with the answers ("50 is 10 times 5"). Occasionally, Pat taps her foot in rhythm to keep the children on track, then returns to her rhythm sticks when it is time to replace the furniture.

The point of the multiplication games has been review, in preparation for a more in-depth division lesson. Using a small slate as her prop and the Sukkot holiday as the theme, Pat leads the children in a discussion of ways that varying numbers of apples might be divided among different numbers of guests. At first, just a few children understand what she is doing, but within a few minutes, hands are going up everywhere. When Pat is satisfied that everyone sees the division process as the reverse of the multiplication they practiced earlier, she has them write the tables they are learning in their class-made practice books.

At last it is time to study the story Pat has written on the board. In large, class-made *main lesson books*, the children turn to the carefully drawn pictures they have made of sukkahs. Now, on the following page, they draw their own light green lines for writing on in preparation for copying the story from the board. Pat is aware that, for some, the copying exercise itself will be a challenge in language learning whereas others could quite easily compose a similar story on their own. It is her intent to maintain group cohesion by keeping them all together for this activity, and she will rely on the more advanced children to help those who may be struggling, thus providing a challenge for everyone while promoting unity.

Just drawing the lines has taken enough time that the 2 hour block is coming to an end. Copying the story will have to wait. It is snack time, and the children know just what to do next: Main lesson books are placed in wooden bins at the edge of the room, chairs are pushed into tables, children stand behind them with hands crossed over their chests, and they then recite together, "There lives in me an image of all that I should be. Until I can become it, my heart is never free." A child lights a single candle and a brief blessing is recited. Then, everyone enjoys the snack they have brought from home along with the day's first opportunity to chat with their friends.

On the way to the recess that follows, one of the girls comes to Pat with a concern. A new student, a boy with no Waldorf background, has been assigned the seat next to her. Michelle explains the frustration of working with someone who seems to make fun of the rhymes and songs. She imitates him briefly then states, "It's really annoying. He just doesn't get it!" Pat reminds Michelle that the boy is new but also agrees that she will talk to him.

For the other 24 children in Pat Tatum's third grade, "getting it" comes easily after being together for more than 2 years. They are not consciously aware of it, but much of Steiner's philosophy for this age group has been demonstrated during the morning's main lesson: children have participated in music, one of the arts, and they have used rhythm and movement to solidify their knowledge of multiplication tables. In addition, the teacher has shown herself the authority when it was time to present new knowledge and demonstrated her sensitivity to a difficult interaction between peers. The Steiner-recommended Old Testament literature has provided an important segment of curriculum content. The class furniture and learning materials have been natural ones, and technology has been totally absent. Finally, awareness of the spirit within has been verbalized by the presnack recitation. In a 2-hour time block, the growth of the whole child, as defined by Rudolf Steiner, has been attended to in one way or another.

For our next visit we enter a very different sort of classroom. Although its teacher shares with the Montessori and Waldorf teachers a desire that children grow to their fullest potential, this teacher approaches the goal from an entirely different direction.

LETTING THE CURRICULUM EMERGE THROUGH CHILDREN'S PROJECTS

A new–old way of teaching young children has been the focus of considerable interest in recent years. With this method, the curriculum is not set but emerges from children's intellectual needs and interests; specific topics and learning experiences are chosen through negotiation among children and teacher. When put together as a whole, the experiences make thematic projects that incorporate many or most areas of the academic curriculum without overtly focusing on one or the other.

The roots of what is now called *the project approach* are in the works and ideas of John Dewey and other similarly inclined American educators, as well as in the *integrated day* or *informal education* adopted by many British schools in the 1970s. In the late 1980s, two North American educators, Lilian Katz and Sylvia Chard (1989) determined that the time was ripe to bring the focused thematic approach back to the forefront of early education. Through workshops, courses, presentations, and a book, *Engaging Children's Minds*, they coaxed teachers to abandon their more traditional ways of teaching in favor of using projects that would stimulate and enhance children's development, both cognitive and social.

Arguing that the best projects are those that help children understand the world that surrounds them, they defined a project as:

> an in-depth study of a particular topic that one or more children undertake. It consists of exploring a topic or theme such as "going to the hospital," "building a house," or "the bus that brings us to school." Work on a project should extend over a period of days or weeks, depending on the children's ages and the nature of the topic. (Katz & Chard, 1989, p. 2)

Although they do not see projects as the whole curriculum, Katz and Chard argue that they are an important complement to standard academics and play. They believe, as did Dewey, that projects help develop a sense of community among the children and that they reflect real life better than does an arbitrary division of the curriculum into discreet subjects. Katz and Chard (1989) even see one aim of the project approach as giving teachers a way to view their work as challenging. They wrote that a "curriculum that limits the teacher primarily to daily instructional lessons or to setting out the same toys and equipment day after day can quickly become dreary and devoid of intellectual challenge" (p. 8).

The Katz and Chard (1989) approach to project learning is more structured than its predecessors, at least in its explanation to teachers. They define three phases in the development of any project:

- *Phase 1* provides time for planning and getting the project off the ground. The teacher can introduce a topic or it can be negotiated with the children. Then, current knowledge is pooled through discussion, dramatic play, drawing, and shared materials from home. This is followed by planning for future study and, perhaps, some preliminary investigations.

- *Phase 2* is the period in which children gain new information by following through on the plans made in phase 1. The teacher guides the children to use research skills appropriate to their age, such as observation and drawing in the earlier years and with writing, reading, and calculating added on for older children.

- *Phase 3* draws everything together as children reflect on what they have learned. Older children might apply their skills in music, drama, dance, various forms of art work, and the creation of class books. They might even invite family members to a presentation. Younger children might reflect primarily through dramatic play, which may help them "integrate their modified and fuller understanding of the real world." (p. 84)

To see how the Katz and Chard vision of project learning can work in an early childhood setting, let's visit a kindergarten–first-grade classroom in which it has been in action for several years.

How One Teacher Applies the Project Approach

When Pam Morehouse, a public school teacher in Washington State, first heard of the Katz and Chard approach to projects, she was excited to learn more. In her K–1 classroom she was already engaged in similar methodology and was intrigued by the structure that they brought to it. Eventually, Pam not only attended Katz's and Chard's summer institute for teachers but began to offer workshops of her own, even presenting with Sylvia Chard.

The first project Pam and her class engaged in after she attended the summer institute was one she was only partially prepared to teach. The children asked her for help in making an airplane that could "fly" in the classroom. Pam is a licensed pilot and could supply the necessary technical information, but she had no background in construction. Fortunately, a local building contractor agreed to help out, accepting as payment the fishing worms the children offered from their compost bin. As the project grew ever more complex, Pam turned to the Boeing Corporation for funding and advice. They, in turn, invited the children to present their finished airplane and their knowledge of flight at a major air show. As a final step, Pam wrote an informative and entertaining description of the project for a national education journal that is read not only by teachers but by principals and superintendents as well (Morehouse, 1995).

A year or 2 later, another group of first graders, with quite different interests, noted with excitement a new building with golden arches rising above the freeway. It was time, they decided, to learn what they could about this kind of restaurant, and so, Pam said, "the inquiry and investigation began."

One indication of the seriousness and respect with which Pam regards her children's interests is her use of the words *inquiry* and *investigation*. In the project approach, even very young children are believed capable of research that is guided, but not directed or taken over, by adults. What does a research project look like when the participants are just 5 or 6 years old? Some of the activities included in the fast-food project were:

• *Classification, by type, of the questions the children generated for their research.* Four categories were defined, and committees were formed to learn about workers, buildings, food, and machines. The children then discussed ways of learning what they wanted to know and decided on first-person interviews, observations, and looking in books.

• *Memory drawings with accompanying stories preceding visits to local restaurants.* The stories demonstrated what the children already knew and remembered about fast-food establishments and inspired questions for upcoming research.

• *Visits to a nearby Dairy Queen and a local drive-in for field research (not just a "field trip," Pam emphasizes).* Here, first-person interviews as well as observations were

When children choose and develop their own projects, they not only participate in role play experiences but in the more traditional curriculum as well.

possible, and each committee had its list of questions to be answered. Topics ranged from length of time it takes to serve a customer to the measurements of each room.

• *A collection of spelling words that began during phase 1 as the children talked about the words they would need to know.* As time went on, Pam wrote individual words generated by the children on small pieces of posterboard and glued to another very large piece that hung on the wall for everyone's reference.

• *Sharing time, in which each committee explained what it had learned in its research.*

• *The grand finale, the creation of an in-class fast-food restaurant.* This was only possible after each committee had shared its expertise with the class and after much hard work to ready the restaurant for customers. Creating a menu and price list required ingenuity and math skills. More math was needed as the children made bills and coins to fill their cash register, then learned to make change with some degree of accuracy. Of course, signs of various sorts had to be created and placed in appropriate places in the carefully designed restaurant facility.

As children took turns being employees and customers, they learned lessons in courteous service. Because their project drew the attention of interested adults, drop-by customers included the district curriculum director, the principal, and university students and professors. Just as previous youngsters had been able to speak to an interested public about their airplane, so were these children able to share their knowledge, with poise and self-confidence. In both cases, they had behind them many weeks of knowledge building, interactions with people in the community, and experiences in both independent and cooperative research. They had been taken seriously by the adults who facilitated their learning, and they had the air of children who expected that such treatment would continue.

In the next section, you learn about a somewhat similar approach to be found originally in Italy and now in a good many early childhood centers in the United States. Differences between the Italian centers and Pam Morehouse's class include the ages of the children (3 to 6 as opposed to 5 to 6), general focus (childcare centers rather than a public school), and adult–child ratios (aides and special resource teachers to assist the regular teacher vs. Pam's assignment as the lone teacher in the classroom). Attitudes toward children and their capabilities and teaching methodology, however, contain striking similarities. After reading about the Italian approach, you visit a U.S. school where many of their ideas have been adapted.

ADAPTING REGGIO EMILIA IDEAS TO A U.S. SETTING

At the end of chapter 2, you were asked to consider what direction your own thinking might take as you progress in your understanding of early development and education. One possibility, of course, is to take the best that each has to offer, thus creating a tool kit of ideas that work. This is the approach that was adopted by an educator from northern Italy shortly after the end of World War II.

Loris Malaguzzi (Edwards, Gandini, & Forman, 1993) was a middle school teacher from Reggio Emilia in northern Italy when, less than a week after the end of the war, he came across a group of parents attempting to build a school for young children. From the rubble of bombed-out buildings, women were finding bricks and washing them by hand; they planned to sell military vehicles left behind by the Germans to finance the rest. Inspired by their vision and determination, Malaguzzi spent the next several years working with the growing numbers of such parent-run schools, all while keeping his position as a teacher and, later, as the founder of a mental health center for children.

By 1963, it had become possible to receive local tax support for the schools, and to this day, parents in Reggio Emilia may choose between sending their preschool children to municipally funded schools, federally funded schools, or private—largely Roman Catholic—schools. It is the municipal schools that are the descendants of those parent-run centers begun with hand-washed bricks and money from German tanks. Until his death in 1994, Malaguzzi was the driving intellectual force behind the development of curriculum and method.

Both he and the teachers made it their commitment to study the ideas of everyone alive or long deceased who might have something of value to tell them. Most of the philosophers and theorists presented in this book's chapter 2, and others besides, provided a foundation for thought and discussion. Because Malaguzzi had been favorably impressed by the Rousseau Institute in Geneva, Switzerland, one of the Reggio Emilia schools' early and important influences was Jean Piaget. Piaget's argument for early exploration in mathematics became an integral part of the curriculum. In addition, his concept of children as builders of their own knowledge or, as Malaguzzi described them, children as "protagonists" in their own learning experiences, was adopted. As time went on, this view of children led to a teaching method much like Katz's and Chard's project approach, although for several years neither knew of the other.

As the Reggio Emilia schools became known to the outside world, explanatory articles and books were published, visitors arrived from around the world to observe and learn, videos showing the children in action were created, and e-mail discussion groups were begun. Despite the intense interest that the Reggio schools have provided in recent years, it remains difficult to describe them in such a way that they can be emulated, because there is no established or approved curriculum and no set of materials to guide one's teaching. This is as it should be, for the core idea of the schools is that they should be flexible, responding to the needs and interests of the children while taking into account the local culture and society. Thus, it would be inappropriate to study these northern Italian schools and then bring their philosophies and practices, without any alteration or adaptation, to the United States.

Nevertheless, there are certain elements contained in the schools that set them apart from most others. Although each of these elements could certainly be found elsewhere, it is the combination of them that makes the Reggio Emilia schools unique. First, they owe much to the ideas about constructivism held by Piaget and Vygotsky, but the ongoing research by teachers and staff ensures that the schools' philosophies undergo continual growth. One example in recent years has been an interest in Howard Gardner's concept of multiple intelligences (and Gardner's interest in Reggio's application of his theory.) Second, a central curricular emphasis is the use of the various arts as a means of communication by children who are, for the most part, preliterate. This emphasis is of such importance that each school is provided with an *atelierista* (art teacher) who works out of his or her own *atelier* (workshop or studio) as well as in the classrooms and in planning sessions with the other teachers. Third, although many of the materials and activities are those that would make any traditional preschool or kindergarten teacher feel at home, there are also in-depth projects throughout the year that are the product of negotiation between children and teachers. These projects may emerge directly from the children and simply be guided by the adults. One example is an amusement park created for the birds that frequented the school playground; this experience was one of such depth and interest that a video was made of it (Forman & Gandini, 1994). There are also projects that are suggested by the teachers, based on their continual observations of the children.

One admirer of the Reggio Emilia schools is Lilian Katz (1993) whom you met in the previous section. She suggests that our teaching of young children could be improved if we gave some thought to the following six lessons she believes these schools can teach us:

- The view of preprimary children in regard to visual representation is that they can "communicate their ideas, feelings, understandings, imaginings, and observations . . . much earlier than most U.S. early childhood educators typically assume." This attitude makes it possible to put art at the core of the curriculum.

- Visual representations are not treated simply as decorative products as they are in the United States. Instead, they are used as resources or reference materials for further study.

- Even though art work is used in such a serious and realistic manner, it does not keep children from being competent in unrepresentative and abstract visual expression as well. In other words, there is art for the sake of artistic expressions as well as art as a substitute for written communication.

- Teacher–child interactions tend to be focused primarily on the content of the children's work and less concerned with daily routines and obedience to rules. In the United States, the focus is more often the reverse.

- Teachers take the children's interests and intellectual efforts seriously and convey their sincere respect.

- The buildings are homelike, with spaces and furnishings designed to "create a comfortable, warm, and cheerful ambience and pleasant environment." (Katz, 1993, pp. 25–32)

To understand how the Reggio Emilia ideas might work in a United States setting, we describe next a school with similar interests and philosophy.

A Visit to the University Child Development School (UCDS) in Seattle, Washington

The school you are about to visit was chosen not because it looks like an Italian Reggio Emilia school (although it does in some respects) but because the philosophy of the directors and teachers in creating learning experiences and curriculum is so like that of the Reggio founders and teachers. The natural outcome is a school that looks very American while adapting much from Reggio Emilia.

Housed in two modest buildings on the fringes of a commercial area, UCDS provides few clues to the casual observer that it is a unique place for young children to play and learn. The entryway, however, provides a visitor the first glimpse of what is to come. Artfully displayed are children's pictures with accompanying (mostly dictated) written descriptions of the development they would like to see in an unused corner of the playground. Amidst them is one larger, similarly focused but adult-made picture by Daron Henry, the resident *atelierista*. The visitor soon learns that the far corner of the playground has recently become available for development with the departure of some materials that had been stored there. The children's pictures and text are the work of individuals, but Daron's picture was created after group meetings in which children shared with him their hopes for places to sit under, climb on, and have games in. They also asked for a place to read "with vines all around."

Once a general plan was decided on, community resources were located that would help the children achieve their goals. For example, the children visited a quarry to choose rocks for a central climb-on sculpture. Back at school, they learned to cement the rocks together with mortar, finally creating a play-on structure with enough similarity to a certain well-known tourist destination for it to be dubbed Kid Henge by the faculty.

Other elements of the playground corner were then added, with children and adults working together to achieve the final design. From start to finish, the project took many weeks and is typical of those experienced by the children at UCDS. As in the Reggio Emilia schools, the children's ideas, concerns, and solutions are received seriously and with respect. As in Reggio, there is an *atelierista* (he prefers the more casual "art-with-Daron"), who helps them visualize and communicate their ideas through graphic representations. In the case of the playground project, the children drew their ideas, discussed them at length, effected appropriate compromises to make the ideas reality, then participated as much as possible in the actual construction. As in Reggio, the children are encouraged to take risks, experiment, and learn from their mistakes. When participating in this or any other project, their misperceptions are not corrected. Instead, the children try out their ideas and hypotheses, then reformulate them as they gain experience and knowledge.

Of course, as in Reggio Emilia, there is much more to the curriculum than projects large and small. The classrooms at UCDS are filled with traditional materials such as blocks and story books, up-to-date resources, such as computers with age-appropriate software, and a schedule that includes snack time and show-and-tell.

Teachers at both UCDS and Reggio learn of children's needs and interests through careful observation and documentation. At UCDS teachers often take photos and write anecdotal notes, and discussions between teacher and child, as well as teacher and teacher, are common. Narrative reports are sent to parents; and, in the near future, remote control videotaping by both children and teachers will be possible.

Directors and teachers are committed to providing the children with an emergent curriculum, that is, a curriculum that emerges from the interests of the children as opposed to one that is stamped out beforehand by adults in authority positions. They are equally committed to an emergent curriculum for themselves and spend much of their time reading new ideas, attending conferences and workshops, and having discussions about techniques and philosophies. Recently, an entire year was devoted to increasing faculty knowledge in mathematics and its teaching. The result is an exemplary approach to math teaching they now share with others through workshops and publications.

The children who graduate from the UCDS early childhood program have one distinct advantage over those in Reggio Emilia. Whereas the Italian children generally move into public schools that are traditional and structured, it is possible for the UCDS graduates to attend another UCDS campus for an additional 5 years of an emergent curriculum taught by teachers who continually seek out new knowledge and who respect their pupils' ideas, interests, and risk-taking efforts.

Project-based approaches, including the Reggio Emilia model in all its variations, are particularly appealing because young children are usually self-directed in their learning, appreciate hands-on activities, and can make connections among a series of events and activities. Some children, however, have difficulty acquiring new skills and knowledge while negotiating the social demands of ongoing activities; others have sensory or physical disabilities that prevent them from moving around and interacting independently with materials and people; still others need specialized instruction to help them focus their attention on learning. Early childhood special education services are important resources for young children who need individualized support to realize the benefits of early education.

HELPING CHILDREN MEET DIFFICULT CHALLENGES: EARLY CHILDHOOD SPECIAL EDUCATION (ECSE)

Until the mid-1970s, children who experienced developmental delays or disabilities were often excluded from public schools, and families were responsible for finding and organizing their children's educational programs, especially for preschoolers. Families who could afford the expense sent their children to special private schools, and those who could not cared for their sons and daughters at home. When families were faced with overwhelming demands in raising children with special needs or could not provide the level of care necessary, the only other option was residential institutions where children often became wards of the state. In the 1960s and 1970s, courageous parents formed advocacy groups and pressed lawsuits on behalf of their children, claiming that denial of public education for children with disabilities was discriminatory. The courts agreed and ruled that children with special needs had the same rights to public education as their typically developing peers.

In 1975, on the heels of many other pieces of civil rights legislation, the United States Congress passed a law requiring local school districts nationwide to provide special education to all eligible school-aged children. This legislation, now known as the Individuals with Disabilities Education Act (IDEA, 1991), represented a remarkable level of commitment for the federal government, since regulation and control of K–12 education had previously been the responsibility of each state.

IDEA legislation has been amended many times, most recently in 1997, and currently mandates special education services for all eligible children beginning at the age of 3. In other words, preschoolers with identified disabilities and delays are the only 3- to 5-year-olds the public schools have a legal responsibility to educate. (States have also been encouraged, but not required, to serve eligible infants and toddlers.)

Eligibility for preschool services can be determined in two different ways. The first is by disability categories that apply to children from age 3 to age 21: mental retardation; hearing, vision, language, or orthopedic impairments; serious emotional disturbance; autism; traumatic brain injury; and specific learning disabilities.

Parents and professionals alike, however, have long voiced significant concerns about premature labeling and misdiagnoses when applying such disability categories to very young children (McLean, Smith, McCormick, Schakel, & McEvoy, 1991). In 1991, Congress added a more appropriate, less specific, eligibility category for preschoolers: developmental delays in physical, cognitive, communication, social, emotional, or adaptive development. This category is strongly preferred to the disability categories for children under the age of 5 (Division for Early Childhood, 1996).

Evaluation of special education eligibility for infants, toddlers, and preschoolers usually involves interviews with parents and reviews of available medical records, as well as a comprehensive interdisciplinary assessment of the child's development. Eligibility evaluation teams generally include a school psychologist, either a speech or motor therapist or both, special educators, family members, and perhaps a social worker. As a preschool or primary teacher, you will no doubt make referrals to special education, and the information and concerns you have about children will prove valuable to the eligibility evaluation team.

Because comprehensive evaluations are quite expensive and time consuming, short screening tests are often given first. If the tests indicate a likelihood of delay or disability, then a full-scale assessment, including both formal testing and observation, is scheduled. Each state defines its own conditions and test scores that qualify children for special education services.

As a preschool or primary teacher, you may well work with children in your classrooms who receive special education services, or you might decide to pursue special education as a career. For our final site visit, let's go to a preschool special education classroom. The classroom is part of the public school system with a program for children ages 3 to 5. Although it is primarily for those who qualify for special education, the class also includes a few typically developing children. (Because of strict confidentiality guidelines in special education, the actual class is not identified by district or teacher.)

The Special Education Preschool

Two preschool children, one boy and one girl, walk confidently into the classroom and look around for the teacher. The little girl's mother calls her back for a quick good-bye kiss, waves at the teacher, and leaves. The children hang their coats and backpacks on hooks under their names.

"Good morning, Lea; good morning, Kyle. How was your weekend? Did you bring your journals?" The children go to their backpacks and produce small hand-bound books with covers decorated in colorful preschool style. Kyle says, "Me wented farm see horse." He seems to have more to say. "Grandma's," he adds after a moment.

"Oh, how fun. You went to your grandma's farm and saw horses." The teacher repeats his sentence using more proper syntax, reads his parents' account of the weekend in the journal, and asks two more questions. Each of Kyle's statements is reflected back to him in extended and expanded form.

Lea stands patiently but expectantly waiting for her turn to show the teacher her journal. She doesn't say any words, but nods, points, and makes some sounds in response to the teacher's questions. Other children enter the room during the next 15 minutes, and by 9:00 A.M. there are seven youngsters present. Most have shared their home–school journals with the teacher, and she has learned that one child was sick over the weekend, one had a toileting accident, and one began drawing pictures for family members. The last two arrivals are talking with the teacher, two boys are building a tower in the block corner, and three girls are using small paper punches at the art table, with help from the teaching assistant when needed, punching out shapes and pasting them on index cards.

At 9:00 A.M. the teacher sings a song about cleaning up. All the children put their materials away and congregate on the rug area in a semicircle around the teacher's chair. Circle time commences with a hello song, each verse greeting a different child. The teacher signs as she sings and most of the children hum, sing, or sign along. The teaching assistant sits behind one boy and helps him follow the motions of the song (pointing, waving, clapping.) The children who are present hang up their name cards on the "In" board and "read" the name card for the child who is absent.

After these traditional early childhood circle-time social activities, the group stays and works briefly on recognizing letter sounds. The teacher starts by using the name cards and asking the group to make the initial sounds of each name as she points to the letter. Some of the children seem to be associating the letters with the sounds; others make the sounds their peers are making.

At 9:20, the speech–language pathologist (SLP) and occupational therapist (OT) come into the room and join the end of circle time while the teaching assistant moves about setting up activities at centers around the room. The SLP goes to the dramatic play center with two children and the OT takes two others to the art table. The teaching assistant goes to the toy shelf with two children who select barn and garage sets, and the teacher works at a small desk with one girl who is learning to recognize numerals. These group activities last 15 minutes, and then the children rotate around to a different adult. After two rotations, the SLP leaves and the children go outside with the teaching assistant.

Outdoor play is a rather rambunctious affair for the first few minutes with much noisy running around before children sort themselves onto tricycles and climbing equipment and to the sand table. Afterward, everyone has a chance to wash hands and help get the snack together. The SLP returns and sits at the snack table, talking with the children and adults, clearly eliciting, expanding, and modeling communication skills. The teacher weaves number, color, time, and size concepts into the conversation as well and reminds children to take turns and share.

Children leave the snack table whenever they are finished, telling an adult the center they will play in next. The two adults cruise from center to center listening, observing, making comments, and asking questions until parents begin to arrive and children depart. The room is quiet as the assistant cleans up and the teacher records each child's progress in individual notebooks. "Every moment counts for these kids," says the teacher. "We are always teaching, even when it just looks like play."

Influences on ECSE Preschools

You have probaby noticed a number of similarities and differences among the special education preschool and the other models described in this chapter. Like Head Start, the ECSE preschool is supported by federal law and funding that flows through

the states to local programs. Both Head Start and ECSE programs are designed to provide support for a particular group of children who are at risk for school failure,
although the eligibility criteria differ. The types of specific materials, structured curricula, and direct instructional strategies found in Montessori preschools can also be
found in ECSE classrooms, sometimes giving an impression of more work than play.
The teachers in ECSE classrooms are more directly responsible for the content and
outcomes of individual children's learning, however. Teaching teams with specialized
expertise are the norm in both ECSE and the Waldorf models, although the particular
specialties are quite different and both models have children with the same teachers
for several years. Project-based approaches are increasingly being modified for use in
ECSE classrooms, with an emphasis on individual education plan (IEP) objectives
that promote repeated practice and generalization of functional skills across a number of related activities. The individualization inherent in the Reggio Emilia model,
along with the partnerships among school, families, and communities, is also reflected strongly in ECSE programs. Perhaps the most important thing to remember about
ECSE programs, however, is that the professionals working in them are familiar with
the full range of approaches in early childhood education, and they work in close partnership with other early childhood programs in the best interests of each child.

EXTENDING YOUR LEARNING

1. Choose one of the models of early education you have studied in this chapter.
   Make a list of the most important elements pertaining to its philosophy or point
   of view. Visit a center or school that represents this model, making notes of
   examples of the philosophy in action.

2. With your instructor, make a list of questions you would like to ask a teacher
   or administrator about each of the models. Singly, in pairs, or in small groups
   of students, interview teachers or administrators in schools that represent the
   models. Compare the responses and discuss possible reasons for similarities
   and differences.

3. Extend your knowledge of the history, philosophy, and ideas of any one model
   by reading the original writings of its founder(s), exploring any studies related
   to the model's effectiveness, or researching government documents for developmental history.

4. Imagine yourself as a well-trained teacher in any one of the models discussed
   in this chapter. List the three or four most important reasons you would choose
   your model. In a small group, share your thinking and listen to others'.

5. Interview parents of children from two or three different models of early education. Explore their reasons for choosing the programs they have and the types
   of parent involvement they experience. Share the results of your interviews
   with your peers who have interviewed parents from other programs.

6. Once you have completed question 4, return to your emerging philosophy of
   early childhood education. What would you change and what would you keep

the same? Use your thinking in question 4 to justify your choices. Add these notes to your developing philosophy.

INTERNET RESOURCES

Web sites provide much useful information for educators and we list some here that pertain to the topics covered in this chapter. The addresses of Web sites can also change, however, and new ones are continually added. Thus, this list should be considered as a first step in your acquisition of a larger and ever-changing collection.

Head Start
    www.acf.dhhs.gov/programs/hsb

The Project Approach
    www.ualberta.ca

Reggio Emilia
    www.cdacouncil.org/reggio-USA

University Child Development School
    www.ucds.org

Vancouver Waldorf School
    www.geocities.com/~vanc_waldorf

VOCABULARY

Anthroposophy.   A term coined by the German Rudolf Steiner. A religious or mystical philosophy that rejects Judeo-Christian theology in favor of the mystical insight of individuals.

Critical or Sensitive Period.   A window of time during which a child is believed to learn a skill or gain an understanding with the least amount of effort and the greatest amount of receptivity.

Developmentally Appropriate Practices.   Teaching practices that take into account a child's developmental stage, individual needs and interests, and culture.

Embryonic Society.   A social structure created by the children in a group, though not fully realized according to adult definition.

Emergent Curriculum.   Curriculum that emerges from children's interests and teachers' understanding of children's needs.

Eurythmy.   A method of teaching dancing or rhythmic movement that includes the recitation of verse or prose, usually with musical accompaniment.

Field Trip/Field Research. A field trip is a learning excursion outside the classroom, generally for no more than one day. Field research incorporates the same idea but emphasizes the learning entailed, particularly as it relates to classroom work.

Practical Life Exercise. A classroom activity in which a task from home life is isolated for the purpose of providing children an opportunity to practice and master the necessary skills pertaining to the task.

References

Barnes, H. (1991, October). Learning that grows with the learner: An introduction to Waldorf education. *Educational Leadership*, 52–54.

Clinton, W. (1997, October 23). *White House conference on child care* [Press release].

Division for Early Childhood. (1996). *Developmental delay as an eligibility category: A concept paper of the Division for Early Childhood for the Council of Exceptional Children.* Reston, VA: Council for Exceptional Children.

Edwards, C., Gandini, L., & Forman, G. (Eds.). (1993). *The hundred languages of children.* Norwood, NJ: Ablex.

Families & Work Institute (1998). www.workfamily.com.

Family Re-Union V. (1996). Press release of proceedings. www.workfamily.com.

Forman, G., & Gandini, L. (1994). *The amusement park for birds* [a video]. Amherst, MA: Performanetics Press.

Ginsburg, I. (1982). Jean Piaget and Rudolf Steiner: Stages of child development and implications for pedagogy. *Teachers College Record, 84*(2), 327–337.

Individuals with Disabilities Education Act of 1990, The. Pub. L. No. 101–476, 105 Stat. 587 (1991).

Katz, L. (1993). What can we learn from Reggio Emilia? In Edwards, C., Gandini, L., & Forman, G. (Eds.), *The hundred languages of children.* Norwood, NJ: Ablex.

Katz, L., & Chard, S. (1989). *Engaging children's minds: The project approach.* Norwood, NJ: Ablex.

Kirschner Associates. (1970). *A national survey of the impacts of Head Start centers on community institutions.* Albuquerque, NM: Author.

Kotzsch, R. E. (n.d.). Waldorf education: Schooling the head, hands and heart. Massachusetts: Author.

McLean, M., Smith, B., McCormick, K., Schakel, J., & McEvoy, M. (1991). *Developmental delay: Establishing parameters for a preschool category of exceptionality.* Reston, VA: Council for Exceptional Children.

Morehouse, P. (1995, May). The building of an airplane (with a little help from friends). *Educational Leadership.*

Schweinhart, L., & Weikart, D. (1993). *Significant benefits. The High/Scope Perry preschool study through age twenty-seven.* Ypsilanti, MI: Author.

Seitel, S. (1998). Frequently asked questions about starting an employer-sponsored, onsite daycare center. *Work and Family Newsbrief.*

Uhrmacher, P. (1995). Uncommon schooling: A historical look at Rudolf Steiner, anthroposophy, and Waldorf education. *Curriculum Inquiry, 25*(4), 381–406.

Washington, V., & Oyemade, U. (1987). *Project Head Start: Past, present, and future trends in the context of family needs.* New York: Garland.

Washington, V., & Oyemade Bailey, U. (1995). *Project Head Start: Models and strategies for the twenty-first century.* New York: Garland.

4

DIVERSITY IN EARLY
CHILDHOOD SETTINGS

*The child is entitled to an education which will promote his general culture,
and enable him on a basis of equal opportunity to develop his abilities, his
individual judgment, and his sense of moral and social responsibility, and to
become a useful member of society.*

Declaration of the Rights of the Child, 1979

▼ *Chapter Objectives*

After reading this chapter, you should be able to:

- ▼ Apply issues of cultural diversity to previously read chapters.
- ▼ Identify characteristics of several U.S. cultures, particularly as they apply to interactions with families and young children.
- ▼ Begin establishing a classroom atmosphere that respects, values, and nurtures all children.

As you think about and apply chapter content on your own, you should be able to:

- ▼ Understand your own culture more fully.
- ▼ Embark on a lifelong process of learning about others' cultures.
- ▼ Collect a bank of ideas for handling diversity issues with skill.
- ▼ Incorporate issues of diversity into your developing philosophy of early education.

Social scientists are forever creating new definitions for that elusive word *culture*, but the one that follows is sufficiently broad for use in this chapter's discussion of early education. *Culture: The knowledge, art, morals, laws, customs, values, attitudes, belief systems, behavioral expectations, and norms that give a society and the individuals in it their identity*. Although we have not yet addressed the issue of culture directly in this book's first chapters, it has been an important presence nonetheless.

For example, in chapter 1, a variety of career options were presented for your consideration. It was important to point out as we did that some of your choices would necessarily be of little financial benefit. In the United States, there has been a strong reluctance to provide government support for the care and education of our youngest citizens. Without such support, living wages for caregivers and teachers, coupled with reasonable tuition rates for parents, has been an impossibility. The cultural values and belief systems that create our philosophical struggle between a desire for freedom from government intrusion and the belief that young children are a valuable asset for the future have yet to be resolved. For now, young children and their teachers remain the unfortunate victims of this cultural confusion.

The historical figures you met in chapter 2 all observed children within approximately the same age range, witnessed approximately the same development and behaviors, yet emerged from their observations with very divergent ideas for education. In great part, these differences can be explained by variations in the cultures of time, place, and people.

For example, Germany in the mid-19th-century was undergoing significant and difficult political developments. Although Friedrich Froebel maintained his distance from politics, he still was affected by changes taking place in his culture. The growing idea that women should have more power over their own lives and his romantic-era reverence for the role of motherhood undoubtedly influenced his belief that providing training for women to be kindergarten teachers was a form of liberation.

It is also significant that Maria Montessori was born just as Italy was unifying as a nation, with an idealism that included new opportunities for females. Equally important was her exile during World War II, forced on her by her unwillingness to cooperate with the dictator Benito Mussolini. It should not be surprising that she created an approach to early education that treated girls equally and included an environment designed to create a predemocratic classroom society.

In chapter 3, we visited several classrooms and centers, some of them influenced by the historic figures from chapter 2, all of them a product, at least in part, of their own cultures. The project approach, for example, provides young children with the power to choose their own curricula, to decide their own methods of learning, and to make decisions as individuals and as groups both large and small. Giving such decision-making power might be dangerous in an autocratic culture; it is more appropriate, even expected, in a democratic society such as the United States.

Reggio Emilia schools grew from an Italian postwar culture of economic desperation and angry pride. Over the decades, the city's infrastructure has been rebuilt, and early childhood educators have expanded their knowledge and altered curriculum and methodology accordingly, all in very Italian ways. Thus, we see the University Child Development School in Seattle (see chapter 3) paying homage to the Reggio Emilia approach in many ways while still retaining its U.S. flavor. For example, there is greater interest in and value placed on, technology. In part, this is due to parental connections with local technology companies, an important component of Seattle's economic culture.

These descriptions of cultural influences are but examples from each chapter. You are invited to discover other ways in which culture has shaped careers in early education, the views of educationists, and the various models of classrooms and centers.

THE ROLE OF IMMIGRATION

Complementary to these influences on early education are the diverse backgrounds of the children who attend the schools and centers. In the United States, such diversity has been growing in recent years as immigrants and refugees enter from an expanding number of countries and our own culture increasingly values the presence of children with disabilities in the regular classroom. Arguing that we must look at the education of young children in new ways, one group of authors summarized the situation, particularly in relationship to immigration:

> The dramatic increase in immigration in the past 20 years, the young average age of immigrants, and the higher birth rate of several of these groups relative to that of white Americans is changing the face of America's people. This rapid demographic change has been called "the browning of America." (Swiniarski, Breitborde, & Murphy, 1999, p. 82)

By the late 1990s, Asia and Africa combined accounted for the largest proportion of immigrants to the United States. When countries were counted singly, however, Mexico was the greatest contributor of new arrivals, with the Philippines a distant second. Perhaps even more telling, the United Kingdom, the original source of American citizens and cultural heritage, was ranked 17th with just 1.5% of the new population. Germany, the leading contributor of new immigrants as recently as the 1950s, did not even make the top 30 countries listed by the U.S. Immigration and Naturalization Service.

From these statistics, it is possible to predict what school and child-care-center populations will look like in the near future. For example, it has been predicted that the 70% White population in 1990s American schools will be reversed by 2026 so that 70% will be non-White. Another prediction is that between 1990 and 2050, the percentage of Whites will fall from 74% to 52% (Swiniarski et al., 1999).

Many people believe it would be a good idea to close the door against the flood of outsiders who want to belong to the American family. The newspapers are full of stories that verify this ongoing sentiment. This is not a new attitude, yet America has always been a nation of immigrants. In the mid-18th century, Benjamin Franklin worried about the influx of African people, fearing the negation of the opportunity to create a society of "the lovely White." In the early to mid-19th century, New Englanders worried about the heavy influx of rural, uneducated Irish fleeing the potato famine. Not much later, there was a nationwide concern about the newly popular kindergartens, which came from a German culture and were frequently taught in German. Would 5-year-olds lose their families' treasured Anglo-Saxon heritage? At the beginning of the 20th century, well-known educational historian Elwood Cubberley (1920/1965) weighed in with his negative opinion of the increasing numbers of immigrants from across Europe as "largely illiterate, often lacking in initiative, and almost wholly without the Anglo-Saxon conceptions of righteousness, liberty, law, order, public decency, and government" (p. 485).

Despite such resentment and prejudice, the vilified groups of the last two centuries have managed to overcome most or all of the barriers erected against them, becoming full participants in the ever-changing U.S. culture. Some members of these groups and their heirs, ironically, have even become strong advocates for keeping out new immigrants. Yet, immigrants continue to arrive, and their numbers steadily increase.

THE DEMISE OF THE MIDDLE CLASS

In a list of 26 industrialized countries, the United States ranks first in the number of millionaires and billionaires, but 18th in the gap between rich and poor children; first in health technology but 18th in infant mortality; first in military technology but last in protecting children against gun violence. A U.S. child, in fact, is 16 times more likely to be murdered by a gun than a child in the other 25 countries combined (Children's Defense Fund, 1998).

By the late 1990s, about 25% of American children were found living in poverty. This means that a rather large proportion of children may arrive at the doorsteps of their centers and schools with insufficient nutrition for effective learning. Their language skills may also be inadequate to meet the middle-class expectations of the school curriculum. Their enthusiasm for learning may be dampened by the anxieties and hardships of homelessness or the distress of untreated illnesses.

As the gap between rich and poor widens and as families from increasingly varied backgrounds move into and across this country, early childhood schools and centers have become ever more diverse. An additional influence on diversity is the recent trend toward including children with special needs in the regular classroom.

THE INFLUENCE OF INCLUSION POLICIES

In the mid-1970s, federal legislation required for the first time that children with disabilities be provided with free public education that was tailored to meet their individual needs. Previously, many children with disabilities stayed at home or went to private schools, and public schools often did not have well-trained special education teachers. This initial special education legislation, the *Education of All Handicapped Children Act* (EHA), followed a number of civil rights cases addressing the rights of racial minority students.

The EHA was quite a landmark, amended 10 years later to include eligible pre-school children (ages 3 to 5) and older secondary students (ages 18 to 21) under the federal mandate for special education services. A few years later, the name of the law was updated to its current *Individuals with Disabilities Education Act* (IDEA). The EHA and IDEA and subsequent amendments address the responsibilities of school districts to eligible students and their families. Most recently, the 1997 IDEA amendments emphasize the involvement of special education-eligible students in the regular classroom curriculum for their grades and require the classroom teacher to be a member of the team that plans and monitors students' individual programs.

The focus of special education services has shifted progressively over the years from exclusion of students with disabilities first to an emphasis on separate, individualized instruction within school buildings, then specialized instruction delivered within the mainstream of classroom and school activities. The diversity in U.S. schools has most definitely been enhanced by inclusion of students with a wide range of abilities.

THE ISSUE OF GENDER

The final aspect of diversity to be discussed here is that of gender. During recent decades, research findings have led to mixed conclusions about the influences on behavioral differences between the sexes. Do girls play in the housekeeping corner whereas boys gravitate to the large blocks because society reinforces such choices or because their biology is sending them preprogrammed messages? Or is it a combination of the two? Full answers have yet to be discovered, but it is known that young children are still developing their sense of biological gender identity as well as their beginning understandings of what societal expectations are for each sex.

Many younger children are not yet sure what makes them boys or girls, believing that the answer may lie in how they dress or in the games they choose to play. In addition, they have an incomplete understanding of biological permanence, sometimes believing that they might change genders as they get older, perhaps even becoming someone else entirely. Parents may not think to explain biological differences to them, or may find the prospect distasteful. Thus, young children take their confusion to school (Derman-Sparks, 1993). Teachers who simply and matter of factly provide them with information about gender help clear up the children's confusions, preparing them for sorting out the pros and cons of societal expectations as well.

> Janice was a mother who purposely chose a female pediatrician for her children so that they would see the normality of girls growing up to take on a traditionally male career. When her daughter Kelly was 4, Janice was startled to overhear her say to the boy visiting from next door, "Okay. You'll be the doctor and I'll be the nurse. Boys are always doctors and girls are always nurses." On reflection, Janice realized that a medical TV show Kelly liked to watch with her parents reflected the more traditional divisions of labor, and she came to understand that society's messages could be stronger than the reality of the child's own life.

We can say that one important goal for any early childhood classroom is "to free children from constraining, stereotypic definitions of gender role so that no aspects of development will be closed off simply because of a child's sex" (Derman-Sparks, 1993, p. 49). At the same time, the example of Janice and her daughter tells us that achieving this goal involves a major commitment of time, effort, and awareness. And the equity value is inconsistent with many culturally defined gender roles and expectations, a situation not always understood or appreciated by families and teachers.

We wrote in chapter 1 about the misperception that teaching young children is easy, perhaps just a form of babysitting. By now it should be becoming increasingly clear that the actuality is much more complex, that the tasks of meeting all children's needs fairly and positively are not easy ones. Yet, it is only in recent years that professionals at all levels have come to realize that the issue of diversity deserves specific and increased attention.

VALUING ALL CHILDREN AND THEIR FAMILIES

In 1987, the National Association for the Education of Young Children (NAEYC) published its first edition of Developmentally Appropriate Practice in Early Childhood Programs (Bredecamp, 1987) and differentiated between appropriate practice for groups of children at particular stages of development and appropriate practice given an individual child's own context. Cultural differences, in the first edition, were deemed a part of variations among individuals. A decade later, NAEYC published a revised edition, with the realization that the original view did not sufficiently take into consideration the strong influence that culture has on children's development and on what and how they learn. "Ignoring or misunderstanding the role of culture in children's development is a serious proposition" NAEYC concluded and

> can lead to many different problems in practice. . . . When the cultural rules of the home and the early childhood program are congruent, the process of learning is eased. However, when the expectations of the cultures of the home and the school or child care program are different or conflicting, children can be confused or forced to choose which culture to identify with and which to reject. (Bredecamp & Copple, 1997, p. 43)

An important role for all teachers and caregivers, then, is to help youngsters bridge the disparities between home and school or center. Not to do so can be damaging to children, in both great and small ways. Many beginning teachers choose to ignore cultural differences, declaring that they love all children the same. The result of this attitude, however, is that the teacher's cultural view tends to be the one imposed on the children, sometimes with a sense of superiority. When teachers convey that their own cultural views are better, the next step may well be to consider children's differences as deficits. "Failing to recognize children's strengths or capabilities, teachers may greatly underestimate their competence. Teachers also miss valuable opportunities to use the full range of children's interests and skills to help them achieve the learning goals of school" (Bredecamp & Copple, 1997, p. 9).

> A teacher educator once looked forward to assigning a practicum student to a particular class of 4-year-olds. The majority of the children were learning English as a second language, seemingly a perfect opportunity for this student, who professed an interest in an international teaching

Girls playing with dolls and boys playing with blocks is a common sight. The reasons for this division have yet to be determined.

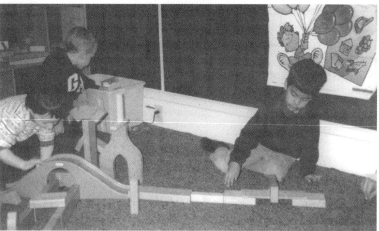

career. Just 2 days into the experience, however, the practicum student began referring to the "language barrier" that was preventing her from teaching anything of value to the children. Her professor discussed with her the fact that the children although beginners at English were already proficient in at least one other home language, and some of them—at just 4 years old—already spoke two. This was a feat that the education student had yet to accomplish, as she only spoke English. Nevertheless, the student continued to focus on the "barrier" that kept her from teaching, and soon she began to speak of the children derogatorily, as "English deficient," seeing the barrier as the children's rather than her own.

Continued work with the student on the part of her university supervisor and the classroom teacher eventually led her to new teaching methods and respect for the children's capabilities, but her original attitude is a common one. Perhaps because teachers have an ingrained disposition to fill in gaps of knowledge, they often look for weaknesses rather than strengths in children. A child who brings another culture and another language to class can be evaluated as having a clearly visible set of deficiencies to be fixed. Yet, it is through honoring the child's abilities and strengths while respecting the family's culture that a teacher can best reach the child. As one writer has said, young children

> deserve to be in programs where it is safe for them to be who they are. . . . Children have the right to feel good about themselves, to learn to be courageous, and not to feel like victims. Children are entitled to their cultural heritage and to be proud of it. (York, 1991, p. 23)

Providing children with the respect they deserve requires that teachers and caregivers know something about the cultural similarities and differences their youngsters bring with them each day. To understand most fully, teachers and caregivers also need to know something about their own cultures. This can be as difficult or more so than learning about another's culture, because our own daily lives have a ring of reality and neutrality, making other points of view seem alien, even unreal. Sociologists describe our unquestioned views as taken-for-granted realities. One example that is frequently given refers to the preference of U.S. mainstream culture to look directly in another's eyes when speaking. This is particularly important when coming across as honest is an issue, or a topic of urgency is being discussed. There are, however, some people who find such physical directness inappropriate, some Hispanic and Native-American cultures, for instance. Thus, a child from one of these groups might look at his feet out of respect for his teacher just when she is saying, "Look at me when I talk to you!" Each person in this unfortunate interchange is, at this moment, in possession of a taken-for-granted reality that is a disservice to the occasion. However, it is the teacher's responsibility, not the child's, to comprehend this and to move to a better understanding of the cultural complexities that make up a classroom.

One aspect of cultural complexity that should be considered is the fact that there is great variability among individual practices and values within any cultural group. Expecting that all Native-American children will look at their feet while the teacher talks, that all Asian Americans will work hard in school, or that all Anglo-European children are programmed for competitive individualism are generalizations of the sort that lead to stereotyping. What is important for teachers in the United States today is "to remember that we must not expect children to learn the same way. Understanding and valuing cultural differences may help us change our teaching strategies to respond more effectively when children are having trouble learning" (Swiniarski et al., 1999, p. 73).

Cultural values commonly held by mainstream Americans include individualism, privacy, equality, informality, wise use of time, achievement, materialism, and directness. Yet, individual Americans, natives and immigrants alike, accept these values at differing levels of intensity. Or, they may fully accept most of the values but completely opt out on one or two (Hanson, 1998). One way to begin handling such complexities in our own teaching lives is to take steps toward a better consciousness of the realities we take for granted, to see our own cultures more clearly.

LEARNING TO SEE OURSELVES MORE CLEARLY

How we see ourselves and our backgrounds has direct bearing on our views of teaching and learning. The first step in dealing with the cultural complexities of teaching is to become consciously aware of our views and the influence they have on our behaviors.

Robin was a first-year teacher being observed by her principal for the first time. For the occasion, she placed the children's chairs in a horseshoe shape and planned a question-and-answer session around a story they were all reading together. The principal sat quietly in the back, taking occasional notes, until she noticed a disturbing pattern. Robin rarely called on any girls, ignoring their raised hands in favor of answers from the boys. Bit by bit the girls began to wilt visibly, their early enthusiasm soon replaced by looks of boredom or resentment. Eventually, Robin began calling on children in what appeared to be a left-to-right order around the horseshoe. The principal breathed a sigh of relief; the girls would finally get a chance. To her amazement, Robin did go around the room in order, but continued to ignore the girls by jumping right over them to call on the next boy. When the principal later brought this to Robin's attention, she denied the possibility that it had happened until the principal showed her the chart she had made of the experience. Together they discussed solutions, finally settling on the idea that Robin make a mental checklist as she called on children, consciously alternating boys and girls as possible.

Caroline, an experienced kindergarten teacher, thought she treated all her children with equality and made sure she gave positive feedback and encouragement in appropriate doses to everyone. One day, a friend on vacation from teaching in another state came to visit Caroline's class. She enjoyed her time with Caroline, but she observed a behavior that bothered her and decided it presented issues that should be discussed. Caroline was stunned to hear that she regularly hugged and touched the White and Hispanic children but not the Blacks. In fact, she couldn't quite believe it and spent the next week in some self-observation and soul searching. Finally, she admitted to herself it was true, realized that it was most probably related to her southern upbringing, and immediately went to work changing her behaviors.

It takes continuing efforts toward self-awareness, and sometimes the observations of a colleague or friend, to prepare ourselves well for handling cultural complexity. A good place to start is to reflect on our own cultural backgrounds, particularly in regard to education. Perhaps you come from a family with many educators in it, so that teaching was a natural choice for you. Or, your family may not particularly value education, but you are pressing ahead anyway, because you believe in the career you have chosen. Perhaps your family takes a different view of education entirely, valuing it for training in specific, hands-on trades and not for the more academic approach you are experiencing. Whatever your family's values and beliefs regarding education, and whether you have accepted or rejected those views, you have been shaped by their influence and will take your attitudes with you into the classroom.

At the end of this chapter, in the section Expanding Your Learning are suggested activities that are intended to help increase your cultural self-awareness. We urge you to try at least one activity. In the meantime, as you have opportunities to work with children, try to observe your own behaviors with boys and girls and with children of different abilities, economic backgrounds, or ethnicities. See if you are drawn to or uncomfortable with one group or another. Then, make specific plans for dealing with your preferences if necessary, so that all children will feel safe and satisfied in their interactions with you.

LEARNING ABOUT OTHERS

In addition to increasing our own self-awareness, an important step in serving children well is to learn something about their cultural backgrounds, particularly if their families have recently immigrated or have influential members—grandparents, perhaps—who help determine the families' views on education and childrearing. This section provides overviews of several cultures commonly found in U.S. centers and schools at the turn of this century. It is important to restate, however, that there are degrees and variations in acceptance of and participation in any culture, even by those who have known only one culture from birth. Additionally, cultures evolve over time, ensuring that some elements may take new forms or even disappear. This is especially true following immigration.

Anglo-European Culture

In the United States, the traditional mainstream culture is Anglo-European. Its roots are seen in documents such as the Constitution and the Declaration of Independence that underlie legal decision making and the rights and privileges that most citizens have come to expect. The culture's roots are also in the nation's mythology of pilgrims seeking religious freedom, patriots fighting their war for independence, and brave families heading west with few possessions but plenty of dreams. Built into this heritage can be found a Puritan work ethic that only permits play once all tasks are done; independent decision making based on enlightened self-interest; and risk taking that allows for failure but generally expects success. Few people today undergo quite the strenuous challenges of these earlier settlers, but their attitudes can still be found, even in an early education setting. The work ethic remains in the requirement that children finish all their work before heading out to recess; independent decision making occurs when learning choices are made by children at centers rather than by teachers; and risk taking is valued when creativity is nurtured.

Other values (Althen, 1988; Hanson, 1998), most of which can be traced back to the country's early days and Anglo-European experience within it include:

• *Equality.* American history is replete with the struggle to live up to this value. From freeing Blacks from slavery to providing women with voting rights, from mandating public education for children with disabilities to grappling with ways to make access to higher education more equitable, the vision of equality continues, slowly, to come closer to reality.

• *Focus on the future, belief in progress and change.* When settling their new land, early Anglo-Americans had few historical frames of reference for what they did; every decision, every move to a new homesite was an act of pioneering. Their descendants carry with them a belief that people are in charge of their own destinies; that progress is almost always possible, given one's own effort and self-confidence; and that change is generally for the good.

• *Respect for action and achievement, inclination toward materialism.* For people focused on progress, change, and self-determination, hard work is, not surprisingly, a concomitant value. Increasingly, the material rewards for hard work have become a strong focus, and the growing materialism that outsiders comment on has become a matter of concern for Americans themselves.

• *Attention to time.* Progress, change, and achievement may come about through hard work, but respect for the clock is seen as an underlying requirement. Value is placed on being on time and on timely efficiency, not only in the work place but in social interactions. Just as it is important to be on the job at the stated starting hour, so it is expected that arrival at a social function won't be much later than the time provided by the hosts' invitation. In the first case, a few minutes early may even be preferred.

• *A preference for informality.* To many outsiders, Anglo-Americans both at home and abroad may be seen to be rude or lacking in class or culture because of their informality of speech and dress. In recent decades, the respect accorded a new acquaintance by using his or her last name has almost entirely disappeared, even for younger children. Jeans and T-shirts are worn everywhere, even on formal occasions. It is possible that such an increase in informality may, in part, be due to the greater emphasis on equality.

• *Communicating with directness and openness.* Subtlety and indirect statements are almost foreign to Anglo-Americans. "What you see is what you get" and "telling it like it is" are valued sentiments in most interactions, and communication of feelings often accompanies a sharing of thoughts and ideas. However, in situations such as talking with a business superior or a new acquaintance, typically Anglo-Americans will be more reticent; moving to the next stage of more open sharing is a sign of increasing friendship.

• *The family.* The nuclear family—mother, father, children—defines the core family for Anglo-Americans. Members of the extended family, who may live at great distances, are referred to as relatives. Although parents do take charge, in America children are also accorded a say in decision making, attaining an early equality not found in many other cultures. The self-determination valued by the larger culture is also manifested within the family, as young adults generally prefer to live outside the home and elderly members also prefer their independence, trying to avoid becoming a burden on the younger generations.

• *Childrearing.* Anglo-American parents essentially begin training their children to grow up and leave home from the time they are born. Newborns are most likely to sleep in their own beds, often in their own rooms. Solid foods are introduced earlier than in some other cultures, and efforts at self-feeding are encouraged and praised. Youngsters may arrive at school wearing mismatched clothing with various fasteners poorly attended to, not because of parental neglect but because the children have been encouraged to choose their own outfits and to dress themselves. In supermarkets and restaurants, young children may be observed making their own choices of foods.

• *Views of illness and disabilities.* Explanations for disabilities generally follow a scientific model that focuses on specific causes: genetic disorders, accidents, disease, prenatal trauma, and so forth. It is believed by most Euro-Americans that better diagnoses, health treatments, education, and living conditions can be of help. The view that the attitudes and behaviors of parents, especially mothers, are responsible for a child's disabilities, for the most part, has faded.

Interactions Between the School or Center and Families

Some cultural customs of Anglo-European Americans are important for teachers to keep in mind (Hanson, 1998). These include:

• Treating people equally, no matter their gender or station in life.

• Freedom of speech on most subjects, although topics related to sex, politics, religion, and physical traits (such as body odor) are typically not discussed in a formal situation.

• People greet each other openly, warmly, and often with a handshake (even if the ensuing meeting is expected to be difficult.) Making eye contact and looking at each other talking indicates honesty and courtesy.

• Except for shaking hands, people do not touch or expect to be touched during interactions with each other. Personal space of about an arm's length is most comfortable.

• Scheduled meetings and conferences are expected to begin on time. If they must be delayed, a brief explanation and possibly an apology are expected.

• Parents generally expect to be informed of their children's progress and are less likely than parents in some cultures to defer to the teacher's expertise and superiority. Parents of children with disabilities are often strong advocates of their children's rights and are aware of the teacher's responsibilities.

• Teachers should expect variations in the Anglo-European culture as determined by section of the country, rural or urban lifestyles, and national or religious heritage. (This is good advice for all the cultures discussed in this chapter.)

African-American Culture

Before Pilgrims landed in what was to become New England, about 20 Africans arrived in Virginia. Like many of the Whites arriving at the same time, they had been kidnapped and sold, then bound to their masters for a set number of years until they had earned their freedom. Blacks and Whites alike were treated abusively, and at times ran away together or bore children together. Either action was punishable, but a subtle difference

When teachers interact with families of cultures other than their own, they will generally have more success if they take time to learn about the families' cultures and communication styles.

in the treatment of the two races set the stage for the imminent move to slavery. In 1640, the Virginia legislature passed a law decreeing that masters should provide firearms to White but not Black servants. The same year, three servants, one Black and two White, ran away and were captured. All three men received 30 lashes, but here the equality of punishment stopped. The White servants were indentured for 4 more years; the Black servant was indentured for "the time of his Natural life" (Takaki, 1993, p. 56). In other words, he became a slave, one of an increasing number during the 1640s. The spread of slavery throughout the Americas led to the forced emigration of 20 million Africans between the 16th and 19th centuries. Of these, 4 million came to North America.

After the American Revolution, in which Black soldiers from each of the 13 colonies participated, slavery was abolished in the northern states. The Civil War in the 19th century may have freed the rest of the slaves legally, but racism continued and grew alongside the increasing participation by Blacks in all aspects of main-stream life. For example, the Ku Klux Klan was organized in 1866, just before the South Carolina House of Representatives found itself with a Black majority. By 1896, the U.S. Supreme Court determined (in *Plessy v. Ferguson*) that states were free to provide separate but equal institutions, and many states, particularly in the South, seized the opportunity, most notably in regard to schools.

Looking for better opportunities, Blacks began to leave the South, only to arrive at the same time European immigrants were also crowding into northern cities. For the most part, help with education, housing, and employment was provided for the

Europeans but not for the African-Americans, who soon settled into city slums. "The impact of prejudice, poverty, and urban ghettos continues to affect many African Americans disproportionately to the present day" (Willis, 1998, p. 169). Yet, by the first half of the 20th century, the exodus of Blacks from the South only grew. Share-cropping in the South was at the whim of floods and insect infestations, and Black farmers found themselves encumbered by increasing debt.

Meanwhile, the influx of Europeans to the North halted during World War I, caus-ing factory managers to send labor recruiters to the South. Widespread institutional-ized racism continued in both North and South until World War II, when the military was desegregated, and even until 1954, when the *Plessy v. Ferguson* ruling was replaced by the Supreme Court's *Brown v. Board of Education* decision, which deseg-regated schools nationwide. In various ways, some of them controversial (e.g., the repeal of affirmative action in some states in the late 1990s), the deinstitutionaliza-tion of racism has continued throughout the remainder of the century. Yet informal or social racism continues. "Negative attitudes, instilled by years of institutionalized breeding of fear and contempt, are still evident" (Willis, 1998, p. 170).

Teachers and caregivers can expect in their encounters with African-American families, to see both the results of this history of maltreatment and the influences of the Anglo-European mainstream culture described in the previous section. Within each family, the extent of these influences will vary, as is the case for any culture and its subsets. The influences and values listed and discussed next reflect an African her-itage but also, at times, input from the U.S. mainstream culture as well.

 • *Language.* The Africans who came to the United States as slaves brought with them a diversity of languages, although there were commonalities within them. It was generally required of Blacks that they learn English, but their interpretation of it was influenced by their native languages. Generations later, some linguistic patterns from these times remain in the speech of many African Americans.

Linguists who have studied the speech patterns of African Americans in recent decades have altered their previous belief that this language is substandard English to an understanding that Black English has its own standardized rules. It has been observed that Black English tends to be used more broadly among people of lower socioeconomic status (SES) and selectively, depending on the social situation, by those of higher SES (Dillard, 1972).

 • *The family.* From the time of slavery, when family members could be sold indi-vidually, to the present day, when single mothers are often the official head of house-hold, the African-American nuclear family has been endangered. In its place has been an extended family model with its roots in African traditions. This heritage has led to a valuing of group effort over private gain. With support from the extended family, however, independence is also valued:

> This may seem at first to be in conflict with the group-effort ethic, but it actually extends that ethic. It has to do with the empowerment that comes when as many as are able can earn a living, meet their family's basic needs, and have a little bit left over to help others in the extended fam-ily who may need temporary assistance. (Willis, 1998, p. 183)

Respect for elders, although eroding in most facets of U.S. society, is historically an African-American value. From Africa came the belief that the oldest members of society are the closest to God; centuries later this idea still leads to the assumption that these are the people who lead prayers in any group setting. Obedience to parents and older siblings has been emphasized more than, for example, the discussions and reasoning often favored by those of Anglo-European heritage.

• *Childrearing.* Guidance from adults has traditionally emphasized discipline and obedience. The African proverb that it takes a village to raise a child is born out in the expectation that extended family and responsible community members will participate in the child's discipline and training. Children are expected to obey the family's rules and treat others with respect as soon as they are old enough to understand. "Although these beliefs are not acted upon by all African Americans because of their life circumstances, they form a core set of beliefs that continue to be valued by many" (Willis, 1998, p. 189).

• *Views of illness and disabilities.* These views vary from an acceptance of the scientific model described in the Anglo-European section to a belief in simple bad luck or misfortune to the view that a child's disability is the result of sinning on the parents' part.

Interactions Between School or Center and Families

Again we emphasize that it is important not to overgeneralize the cultural influences on any one group. Some ideas to think about with that necessary caution, however, include:

• Communication is likely to be "high context," that is, less verbal and more through shared history, facial expressions, and other body language.

• Emphasis may be placed more on the situation than on time. Thus, it is more important to finish the business of a meeting than to watch the clock.

• Addressing parents and other adults by their last names and titles until invited to use the first name is considered polite. Not to do so indicates disrespect.

• Telling ethnic jokes of any kind should be avoided. African Americans often feel as though the joke would be about them if they were out of the room. (This is good advice for all teachers at all times with all cultures.)

• If an African-American child lives with an extended family, it may be someone other than or in addition to a parent who is responsible for home–school communication and who should be invited to conferences and special events.

Native-American Culture

It is estimated that before Europeans began to explore and settle North America, the Native-American population numbered about 5 million. By the 1800s, warfare and infectious diseases brought by White settlers had caused a drop to just about 600,000 people. The great loss of population led to a weakening of tribal alliances, leaving an opening for aggressive European advancement.

From the Native-American point of view, interactions were more or less negative, depending on the motives the outsiders brought with them. For the French, economics was the driving force. Trappers and traders lived with the Native Americans, learned from and worked with them, and sometimes married them. The English looked more toward building permanent settlements in their own style. Native Americans were at times viewed as impediments to success and were thought of as savages and pagans, scarcely worth noticing unless it became necessary to remove them from the land that the English claimed for their king. The Spanish, like the French, brought economic motives but were swayed more by valuable metals than by furs. In addition, they expended their energies spreading their Roman Catholic faith through the establishment of a system of missions. Native Americans became a source of free labor as well as potential Christian converts. Faced with the powerful English and Spanish forces of expansion, the Native Americans lost hope for keeping either their land or their culture, and for the most part, they lost both.

As the United States began to form a nation, then expanded geographically, policies toward Native-American populations fluctuated wildly. Throughout much of the 19th century, negotiations took place by treaty. By the end of the century, tribes were relocated to reservations on lands deemed undesirable for the ever-growing numbers of settlers. "Such forced relocation not only broke the spirit of many once-proud Indian nations, but also destined them to a life of poverty and hopelessness—conditions that continue to haunt Native Americans today" (Joe & Malach, 1998, p. 130). The 1990 United States Census found that 38.8% of Native-American children were living below the poverty level as compared to 12.5% of Whites and 32.2% of Hispanic children. Only Black children fared worse, at 39.9%.

Toward the end of the 19th century, the government decided that individual land ownership would make the Native Americans more civilized, more productive, and more American. The reservations were carved up into individual plots under the Dawes Act of 1887, with any leftover land reverting to the government for more settlement.

By the 20th century, fewer than 250,000 Native Americans were left in North America. Government policies began to focus ever more on assimilation into the mainstream culture. Children were removed from their families and sent to boarding schools, sometimes forcibly. They were punished for speaking their native languages, sometimes by physical cruelty, and denied ties to their home cultures. In the 1960s and 1970s, a time of upheaval nationally, Native Americans across the United States began to demand the return of federal surplus land and the rights given to them by long-dishonored treaties. Such events as the occupation of Alcatraz island and the takeover of the Bureau of Indian Affairs in Washington, DC, drew attention to the continuing plight of Native Americans. Some reforms began to be implemented and included the Indian Health Care Improvement Act of 1976 and the Indian Child Welfare Act of 1978. The former provided extra resources for improving Native American health both on and off the reservation; the latter gave tribes greater power over placement of children put up for adoption.

Today, children are no longer forced to leave home for boarding schools. They may attend public schools or those provided on their reservations. Too often, those attending public schools have not been treated well. Even when much energy is devoted to making school a welcoming place, parents may be reluctant to participate in any way, recalling all too well the pain of their own experiences.

As you think about interacting with Native-American families, consider the cultural values discussed next. Keep in mind that they will be held to different degrees by people who live on reservations or in urban settings and will be somewhat different from tribe to tribe.

• *Group orientation.* Tribal affiliation is an important aspect of identity. Some Native-American languages do not include a word for *I*. Group consensus is important in decision making, and everyone involved is permitted to speak. Decisions may not be made on the spot but are deferred until everyone has had time to think things over. Aggressive and competitive individualism are usually rejected; children who develop these qualities from the mainstream culture may be taunted by their peers (Joe & Malach, 1998). Mainstream teachers may mistake the more typical quiet, self-effacing behavior as evidence of passivity or laziness.

• *Acceptance of events.* Members of the mainstream culture tend to focus on taking charge of, or doing something about, negative events or natural disasters. The Native-American approach tends more toward acceptance of the situation "as part of the nature of life and that one must learn to live with life and accept what comes, both the good and the bad" (Joe & Malach, 1998, pp. 140–141).

• *Self-reliance.* Parent-to-child teaching style occurs largely through modeling and direct telling. As children observe their parents in action, they learn quickly about expectations of the adult world. One cross-cultural study (Miller, cited in Joe & Malach, 1998) showed that whereas White and Black children were expected to do regular chores after they reached age 6, Native American children did so at less than age 5½. Native American children learned to dress themselves earlier as well, at 2.8 years old as opposed to almost 4 years old for White and Black children.

• *Time orientation.* Time for many Native Americans is more flexible than for people in the mainstream culture. Keeping to the dictates of the clock is not nearly so important as making sure that a meeting or conference is finished satisfactorily for all parties.

• *Language.* During the years that assimilation was emphasized, tribal languages began to disappear. Today, there is a widespread effort to reclaim nearly-dead ancient languages. Some schools, including Head Start centers, begin early to teach children both the native culture and language as well as mainstream culture and English.

• *The family.* The extended family is frequently important for Native Americans living on reservations, but the nuclear family is more commonly found in urban areas. In extended families, grandparents or other relatives may take a major role in raising young children if the parents are working. It is important for a teacher or caregiver to understand each family's situation before conferring about the welfare of their child.

• *Childrearing.* The extended family may assign different roles to different members. In some tribes, grandparents may provide spiritual and cultural guidance and uncles may handle discipline (Joe & Malach, 1998).

Traditionally, Native American children were not disciplined with corporal punishment. They were generally introduced to this approach during the often-abusive years in boarding schools run by the mainstream culture. Their years away from home kept Native-American children from learning parenting skills either from their own culture or from the mainstream culture, whose homes they rarely observed. There are attempts during this generation to heal the wounds of the past and to return to more traditional ways.

• *Views of illness and disability.* Although Native-American families may accept a scientific explanation and treatment of children's sickness and disabilities, they may also turn to their culture to explain the reasons for the problems as well as for additional treatment ideas. Causes such as witchcraft, spirit loss or intrusion, or spells may be considered important influences. Parents may wish to consult with a tribal healer before or during mainstream treatment (Joe & Malach, 1998).

Interactions Between School or Center and Families

Remembering again that acculturation varies across families and situations, a number of suggestions can still be made for school–family interactions based on Native-American history, traditions, and present-day culture (Joe & Malach, 1998; Krogh, 1994).

• Before a conference, ask parents which family members should be included. They may or may not wish to bring others. If several people do come, be sure to address and listen to them all.

• Avoid intimidating family members; listen to their ideas and ask questions rather than lecturing to them. Ask them what they see as their child's special talents and gifts.

• Visit the children's homes or reservation. Be a part of the community from time to time by being knowledgeable about holidays and perhaps participating in special events.

• Respect the family's preference for bicultural or bilingual education for their child.

• Take time to learn about the communication style of the Native-American culture in your area. You may need to become more reserved and quiet during meetings than you typically are.

Latin-American or Latino Culture

Today there is concern in much of the United States about illegal immigrants crossing the border from Mexico, but a century and a half ago the situation was reversed. Then, California, Texas, New Mexico, Arizona, and Colorado belonged to Mexico. But, as one Mexican of the time complained, Americans had "formed for themselves"

Games and play are central to cognitive and social development in the early years and are frequently used to promote cross-cultural interaction.

the idea "that God made the world and them also, therefore what there is in the world belongs to them as sons of God" (Takaki, 1993, pp. 172–173). This view was corroborated by the statements and actions of Americans, from presidents to ordinary citizens, many of whom simply moved illegally into Mexican territory. Americans declared it their *manifest destiny* to control the major portion of the North American continent and, by the end of the Mexican War of the 1830s and 1840s, did just that. Suddenly, the northern half of Mexico belonged to the United States, and the area's residents found themselves with a choice of heading south or remaining as potential U.S. citizens. Most chose to stay and before long found themselves facing increasing antagonism toward their language and culture on the part of the growing Anglo-European population. The hunger for ever more land also ensured that eventually even the richest Mexican-California landholders were stripped of everything they owned.

Many in the United States today have chosen to forget this past, but those of Mexican heritage have not. Similarly, there is a general tendency to regard most Mexican Americans as immigrants although many can trace their ancestry in the area to the 1700s or earlier.

In the Southeast, particularly in Florida, the greater impact has come from Cuba, the Caribbean island the United States attempted to buy from Spain in the 1850s, then fought over five decades later. Making Cuba a U.S. colony was, at times, on the political agenda but, in the end, it retained its independence.

At the very end of the Spanish-American War, even as the final treaty was being delivered for signature, the United States managed to overtake Puerto Rico and keep it for its own territory. Today, immigration comes from both Cuba and Puerto Rico, but in very different fashions. Because Puerto Ricans have U.S. citizenship, they may travel as they please, usually to find more economically satisfying work, then return home, just as any other citizen might do. Cubans, on the other hand, have arrived as refugees in periodic waves since Fidel Castro's revolutionary takeover in 1959. Because the first wave of refugees came from the educated upper classes, the Cuban story has been one of greater economic success than has generally been true for Puerto Ricans and Mexicans. The development of Miami as an international trading center has been, to great extent, the result of the efforts of Cuban exiles.

Although less noticeable, because they have not settled in an easily identifiable area, immigrants from Central America have also been changing the face of the United States in the past generation. The teacher or caregiver involved with families from the various Latino cultures needs to realize that there are a number of differences among them, just as there are within each of the cultures we discussed previously. It is not only geographical difference that must be taken into account but class differences as well. To a great extent, the Latin-American tradition has included notable separation of the classes. At the top are those who claim Spanish ancestry; far below are the *Mestizo* (mixed), Black, and Native classes. A middle-class immigrant family from Mexico City, for example, might well have more in common with the U.S. mainstream culture than with a U.S.-born Mexican family of low-socioeconomic status (Zuniga, 1998). Often, immigrants remain more conscious of their class status than people of the mainstream culture realize.

Although it is difficult to assign a single set of values to a cultural group with so many variations in its subcultures, several attributes can be listed for teachers and caregivers to consider (Zuniga, 1998).

- *Machismo and a changing patriarchy.* Traditionally, Latino culture has valued strong leadership on the part of the father. In the past generation, this has been changing, as more women enter the workforce and become more highly educated. The tradition remains in many ways and in many families, however, and it is most courteous to speak to the father first if both parents are present at a conference or meeting.

- *Personalismo.* Warm interpersonal interactions are valued over the task orientation of the mainstream culture. Beginning any encounter with some informal chatting helps establish a good working atmosphere and may go a long way toward establishing trust of the teacher or caregiver.

- *Time.* Interpersonal relationships are more important than retaining an inflexible timetable. It is important to avoid giving parents the feeling that you are impatient or always in a rush, connoting that you don't care about them.

- *Language.* It should not be assumed that Spanish is the first language of all immigrant families. A growing number of them come from areas where indigenous languages are prevalent, and they may not be completely fluent in Spanish.

Communication is generally high context, making body language and attitude as important as the words spoken. Teachers should take care to communicate in all ways their acceptance and respect.

• *The family.* Although the urban family headed by a single mother is a growing phenomenon, Latino families have maintained a far lower divorce rate than have other cultures, a fact that may well be related to the continuing influence of the Roman Catholic religion. Extended families traditionally have predominated.

• *Childrearing.* In general, children are viewed as the prime reason for marriage and as the validation of it. A relaxed attitude is taken toward early achievement, with more focus on nurturing and indulging a young child. Both physical and emotional closeness prevail among all members. Identity with the family rather than independence is nurtured throughout the child's growing up years. Cooperation rather than individualism is generally valued. In poorer families, children may be expected to pitch in by taking on work roles fairly early.

• *Views of illness and disability.* Middle-class, acculturated families may well have adopted the Anglo-European scientific views described previously. Others may bring with them a folk tradition as well as influences from the Latino Catholic church, which also incorporates many folk traditions. Thus, a disability may be seen as a curse from some present evil force. Belief in a punishing God and in the inevitable tragedy of life may lead to an accepting and fatalistic view of a disability or chronic illness.

Interactions Between School or Center and Families

Some suggestions that may be helpful across the various Latino cultures include:

• Always begin interactions with some informal conversation; avoid the temptation to get right down to business.

• Tone of voice and body language are important. Avoid coming across as authoritarian, tough, and harsh.

• Try not to appear hurried and impatient. Let the parents know that you are listening and that you care.

• If both husband and wife are present, speak to the husband first. Unless it becomes apparent that they have adopted a more mainstream family structure, continue to defer to the husband as the family leader.

• Communicate your delight in and affection for their children as a centerpiece of, rather than a sideline to, the discussion.

Asian-American Cultures

The fastest growing ethnic minority group in the United States in recent years has been Asian, with a population of about 3.5 million in 1980 expanding to around 10 million in 2000 (Chan, 1998). Of the cultural groups discussed in this chapter, those of Asian influence are, perhaps, the most varied. The inability of many Americans to tell Chinese from Japanese or Thais from Vietnamese indicates a need to become more knowledgeable rather than any actual lack of difference between the nationalities. As one Chinese immigrant's son argues, the perception that Asian immigrants are all much the same or, at least, mysterious, "serves to disguise the reality of unique customs, traditions, values, beliefs, and familial systems based on political and religious foundations that are thousands of years old" (Chan, 1998, pp. 252–253). Most pertinent for our purposes, a lack of knowledge may lead a teacher or caregiver to misunderstand the feelings that children's families have toward one another—feelings that may be based on centuries of conflict or friendship.

Over the years, immigration from Asian countries to the United States has been affected by two general influences: changing U.S. immigration policies and difficulties in various Asian countries, such as economic hardship and wars. This section discusses these influences on immigrants from two countries. Further research into the experiences of other peoples will broaden a teacher's ability to work well with families from other cultures as well.

Chinese-American History

Widespread famine, economic depression, and civil wars in mid-19th-century China, coupled with the news of recently discovered gold in California, caused the first major influx of Chinese people to the United States. The plan for most of these men, who came by the tens of thousands, was to mine for 3 to 5 years, then return home with enough money to retire on. A very few were able to do just that, and so the legend of *Gam Saan* (Gold Mountain) continued to grow, despite the fact that most of the Chinese did not do well and had to find more menial jobs to survive. Soon, many of them were hired by private companies contracted to extend the national railroad system to the West Coast. The Chinese proved to be excellent workers who cost less than U.S. citizens, a situation almost guaranteed to lead eventually to resentments and disputes.

The result was the Chinese Exclusion Act of 1882, the first federal law that banned an entire nationality from entering the United States. It was not repealed until 1943. The years between found some Chinese returning home but many others remaining to face institutional and violent racism. To avoid deportation, it was generally necessary to change one's status from laborer to businessman. The creation of urban Chinatowns provided some cultural security, safety from racism, and business opportunities, and many of these cities within cities remain today.

Due to a rigid quota system, it was not until 1965, with the passage of the Immigration and Nationality Act Amendments, that a second wave of Chinese could enter the United States. Since preferred status was given to educated, professional, and skilled workers, this second group provided a new stereotype of Asians as overachievers. Their children and grandchildren are still labeled today with the expectation that they all will be the best performers in their classes.

Chinese-American Language

The Chinese are connected by a single written language, but the pronunciation of its pictographic characters varies widely across dialects. Chinese contains many monosyllabic words that are often differentiated by the pitch, or tone, of pronunciation. Word order is different from that of English, and there are no tenses, plural endings, or verb conjugations. Imagine the total reorientation to language that every Chinese immigrant child and parent must undergo when learning English!

Vietnamese-American History

Although Vietnam's northern border touches China, and many of its original inhabitants are thought to have come from southern China, the country's culture and language have evolved quite differently in many ways. China ruled the country for about 1,000 years, but beginning in 111 B.C., numerous rebellions led to independence that lasted until the French colonized Vietnam, from 1883 to 1954. During World War II, the Japanese occupied the country and, this time, rebels adopted Communism. After the war, the French tried to regain control but managed only to retake the south while the Communists controlled the north. With the French finally repelled from the south as well, the country was officially divided between north and south, both sides claiming exclusive power over the entire country. By 1960, war was in full swing with the Soviet Union and China aiding the north and the United States supporting the south.

During the 20 years of the Vietnam war, many South Vietnamese put themselves at risk to aid the U.S. troops. As the south and its U.S. allies lost the war, many South Vietnamese were forced to flee. Over time, more than 1 million became refugees in both Asian and Western countries, primarily in France and in the United States. These ranged from educated professionals to Hmong people from remote mountain areas and to "boat people" who had survived extraordinarily horrific conditions. Immigration policy has been to disperse the Vietnamese throughout the United States rather than permitting "Vietnam-towns" to develop. Thus, in almost any area of the country, teachers and caregivers may encounter second- or even first-generation Vietnamese immigrants.

Vietnamese-American Language

Like Chinese, Vietnamese is tonal, contains many monosyllabic words, and has no plurals, tenses, or verb conjugations. Originally, written Vietnamese was based on the Chinese system but, since World War I, the Roman alphabet, with several additional tone marks, has been adopted.

Shared Values

Although their societies have developed in some differing ways, Chinese and Vietnamese also share values that are similar, with roots that go back thousands of years. Thus, the following cultural traits can generally be applied to both.

- *Family.* The Asian family as the central focus of the individual's life "engenders primary loyalty, obligation, cooperation, interdependence, and reciprocity" (Chan, 1998, p. 292). In Asian cultures, the individual is believed to be today's extension of a family that goes back to the beginning of time. Thus, there is as much thought for the past as for the present. Both the Chinese and the Vietnamese adhere to the ancient Confucian hierarchical system in which the father has primary leadership within the nuclear family but living grandparents are at the top of the extended family.

- *Harmony.* "The keynote of existence is to reconcile divergent forces, principles, and points of view in an effort to maintain harmony. The individual must strive to achieve intrapsychic harmony, interpersonal harmony, and harmony with nature as well as time" (Chan, 1998, p. 293). Asian Americans guided by the tradition of harmony avoid confrontation; demonstrate constraint in verbal, social, and emotional interactions; help others save face by showing respect; and value politeness and tact. A teacher or caregiver with a tendency toward extreme directness should keep these characteristics in mind in order to help interactions with more traditional Asian Americans to succeed.

- *Patience and endurance.* Along with patience and endurance, industriousness and tolerance have provided strength to Vietnamese and other southeast Asians who have lived through subjugation, war, and great loss. For the Chinese, it has been important to persevere quietly, without complaint. For many Asian Americans, it is bad form to share problems with someone such as the teacher. They may even smile and assure everyone that everything is just fine, thus politely sparing others the need to share their pain.

- *Childrearing.* Having children is the cement of marriage, more important than the relationship between husband and wife. During a child's infancy, loving parents are permissive, tolerant, and ready to answer every discomfort. Breast feeding may last 2 years or longer, but toilet training may begin after just a few months, although it is not coercive. The indulgence of the early years is replaced, once school age is reached, with an expectation of self-discipline, responsibility, and a better understanding of adult mores and roles. Whereas the early years are characterized by guidance from the mother, the father now participates in childrearing as well, and disciplinary expectations are increased.

- *Views of illness and disability.* Families that have recently immigrated may well retain traditional views that conflict with the Anglo-European scientific model. A child's good behavior and success in school are viewed as the family's responsibility. Thus, a child with a behavior disorder or mental retardation can become a source of embarrassment for the family, someone who just needs more support from home. A mother's behavior during pregnancy may be seen as the cause of a disability, including such things as eating taboo foods, engaging in reckless or inappropriate activities, or using tools, particularly scissors or knives.

Interactions Between School or Center and Families

Asian cultures can vary widely, but some suggestions may prove helpful in your interactions:

- In communication, body language is much more subdued than in other cultures, e.g., Anglo-European, African American, and Latino. Speaking with great animation may be overwhelming and turn off useful exchanges. Emotional restraint and general reserve will be received with more comfort.

- Sustained eye-to-eye contact is considered rude and should be avoided.

- Until you know the parents well, avoid asking personal questions about their lives. This even includes asking their opinions on politics, which for many Asian cultures is akin to asking pointed questions in the mainstream culture about religious preference.

Some General Conclusions

There are in the United States today numerous ethnicities, cultures, and nations of origin. It is impossible within the confines of this single chapter to do more than touch on a few. We hope, however, that the descriptions provided here may give the reader two directions for further learning: a better realization that knowledge of child and family background can go far toward positive family interactions and progress in learning; and a better understanding of one's own culture. If your culture was represented in one or more of the descriptions, were there items that surprised you but rang true? Were there some that did not seem quite right? Should others be added? As we delve further into the attributes of our own and others' cultures, we gain appreciation of our common humanity as well as greater skill in providing the most positive atmosphere for the intellectual, emotional, and social growth of all the children entrusted to us.

It is important to learn about and respect other cultures, abilities, and viewpoints; yet doing so is not sufficient to move our society forward. It is also important to realize that biases develop very early in children's lives, thus making it a clear responsibility of early childhood educators to be proactive in their classroom responsibilities.

BEING PROACTIVE IN THE CLASSROOM OR CENTER: AN OVERVIEW

Later books in this series will provide practical applications for the information contained in this chapter. Here, our goal is to provide some introductory considerations for the reader who is beginning to interact with children and families from a variety of backgrounds. We hope that an atmosphere of acceptance, caring, and concern for all children will imbue the reader's teaching goals. As you think about ways to make all children feel welcome and valued, it is essential to have some underlying goals that guide your everyday interactions. The following list is adapted from three books that have proved helpful to many teachers (Derman-Sparks, 1993; Ramsey, 1987; and York, 1991).

Teachers should:

- Recognize the beauty, value, and contribution of each child.

- Provide children with accurate, developmentally appropriate information.

- Encourage young children's openness and interest in others, willingness to include others, and desire to cooperate.
- Promote effective and collaborative relationships with children's families.

Children should:

- Develop positive gender, racial, cultural, class, and individual identities.
- See themselves as part of the larger society, identifying with and relating to members of all groups.
- Learn to respect and appreciate the diverse ways in which other people live.
- Feel pride but not superiority in their racial identity.
- Feel free to ask about their own and others' physical characteristics; about issues of racism, ability, culture, gender; and about current events.

Suggestions for achieving these goals include:

- Look carefully at the room's materials for play. Do they respect and reflect the cultures of all your children? Commercial tools for the housekeeping corner, for example, typically reflect middle-class, Anglo-European values.
- Scan all books to see if pictures represent varying ethnicities, ages, and abilities. Are both genders engaged in nontraditional as well as traditional roles? Are there pictures of wheelchairs, eyeglasses, walkers, hearing aids and so forth?
- Decorate the walls with photographs of people from various cultures, ethnicities, and abilities. Discuss them informally with the children.
- Balance individually oriented activities with cooperative learning experiences.
- Display alphabets, labels, and quotes from different writing systems. Teach a few words or numbers in different languages, particularly those represented by cultures in the classroom.
- Avoid pictures, dolls, and activities that stereotype or misrepresent other cultures: festival clothes presented as though they are worn all the time; historical representations presented as if they were current; teaching about a country of origin to explain about their U.S. descendants (e.g., Japan to learn about Japanese Americans.)
- Avoid studying ethnic or cultural groups only at high-visibility times (e.g., Blacks for Martin Luther King's birthday, Native Americans at Thanksgiving.)
- Do not ignore children's discriminatory comments or behavior—they will not go away. Rather, make rules about the treatment of others, then intervene immediately if necessary, just as you do with any misbehavior. Teach about feelings, friendship, respect, citizenship, stereotypes, and differences.
- Listen to your own speech and observe your own interactions. Do you speak with a harsher tone of voice for some children than for others? Do you touch

some children less than others? Are you more inclined to take disciplinary action toward some?

In this chapter we discussed the need for all children to feel welcomed and valued in our classrooms and centers. We described several cultures commonly seen in the United States today and the ways in which their members might look at their experiences in and out of the classroom environment. We also considered a few practical ways to incorporate a respect for diversity in the classroom or center. Finally, we should point out that given the multicultural nature of today's world, diversity is an important issue for all teachers, not just for those who teach in a diverse classroom. All children deserve opportunities to learn about the complex world around them.

EXTENDING YOUR LEARNING

1. Visit a school or center with several languages represented. Interview teachers and observe the ways in which non-English-speaking children are introduced to their new language. Find out how children's needs are cared for when linguistic communication isn't possible.

2. Recall your first introduction to differences in gender, race and ethnicity, ability, and social status. How did you respond to your new knowledge: Was the experience positive, negative, or mixed? Do you have uncomfortable memories of your own actions or of those of others to children who were different in these ways?

3. Think about the views of your family members concerning differences in gender, race, ability, and economic status. Do you generally accept them? Reject them? Can you explain why?

4. Choose a country about which you know little, one that has children registered in schools and centers in your area. First, do some library research about that country's history, geography, and culture. Then interview two or more parents (or grandparents) from that country about their views of education. Consider how you could adapt your curriculum or methodology to meet their children's needs from the family's cultural point of view while still providing the skills the children will need to survive well in the mainstream culture.

5. Start a file box of ideas for your classroom that incorporate ways to handle diversity issues. You might have a section for each area of the curriculum, another for parents, and another for the environment.

6. During your student-teaching experience, invite all parents to participate and share in classroom activities and outings. Have parents teach songs or read picture books in their native languages.

7. Has your thinking changed, or perhaps been solidified, pertaining to cultural issues and your teaching? Reflect on your feelings as you read this chapter and what they will mean to you in your teaching. Add these ideas to your personal philosophy notes.

8. Take advantage of opportunities to attend and participate in public events sponsored by cultural groups other than your own. Accompany families, if invited, to traditional healers, holiday celebrations, family gatherings. Note the aspects of each event that are familiar and comfortable as well as those that are unfamiliar and uncomfortable for you.

INTERNET RESOURCES

Web sites provide much useful information for educators and we list some here that pertain to the topics covered in this chapter. The addresses of Web sites can also change, however, and new ones are continually added. Thus, this list should be considered as a first step in your acquisition of a larger and ever-changing collection.

Anti-Bias and Conflict Resolution Curricula: Theory and Practice
www.ed.gov/databases/ERICDigests/ed377255.html

Anti-Bias Curriculum: Books for Young Children
http://web.nmsu.edu/~gpeterse/book2.html

Children's Book List-Disabilities
www.math.ttu.edu/!dmettler/dlit.html

Culturally & Linguistically Appropriate Services Early Childhood Research Institute
http://clas.uiuc.edu

Early Childhood Education
www.ecewebguide.com/antibias.html

Educating Language Minority Children
http://ericeece.org/pubs/digests/1990/bowman90.html

Global Classroom
www.global-classroom.com

The Global Schoolhouse
www.gsh.org

Immigration and Naturalization Service
www.ins.usdoj.gov

Meeting the Diverse Needs of Children
www.ncrel.org/sdrs/areas/issues/students/earlycld/ea400.html

Multicultural Book Review Homepage
www.isomedia.com/homes/jmele/homepage.html

Multicultural Pavilion
http://curry.edschool.Virginia.EDU/go/multicultural

People of Every Stripe
www.teleport.com/~people

Selecting Culturally and Linguistically Appropriate Materials:
Suggestions for Service Providers
   http://ericeece.org/pubs/digests/1999/santos99.html

World Wide Holiday E-Mail List
   www.go-global.com/Free.html

VOCABULARY

High Context Communication.   Communication between people that emphasizes non-verbal signals such as body language.

Indentured Servant.   A person under contract binding him or her, as a laborer, to another for a given length of time. In the early American colonies, an immigrant so bound.

Low Context Communication.   Communication between people that emphasizes verbal language at the expense of non-verbal signals.

Manifest Destiny.   A U.S. doctrine of the 19th century in which the country's continued territorial expansions was postulated to be obvious and necessary.

Separate but Equal.   Until 1954, when overturned by the U.S. Supreme Court, a doctrine that racial segregation in schools and other facilities was constitutional as long as the facilities were about equal for both Blacks and Whites.

Multicultural.   Containing many cultures. In education, the focus is on appreciating the contributions of all cultures.

Taken for Granted Realities.   Elements of a culture that are so embedded as to be invisible to the members of the culture as anything other than realities that are believed to pertain to all humans.

References

Althen, G. (1988). *American ways: A guide for foreigners in the United States*. Yarmouth, ME: Intercultural Press.

Bredecamp, S. (Ed.). (1987). *Developmentally appropriate practice in early childhood programs serving children from birth through age 8*. Washington, DC: National Association for the Education of Young Children.

Bredecamp, S., & Copple, C. (Eds.), (1997). *Developmentally appropriate practice in early childhood programs*. Washington, DC: National Association for the Education of Young Children.

Chan, S. (1998). Families with Asian roots. In E. Lynch & M. Hanson (Eds.), *Developing cross-cultural competence* (2nd ed.). Baltimore: Paul H. Brookes.

Children's Defense Fund. (1998). *The state of America's children: Yearbook 1998*. Washington, DC: Author.

Cubberly, E. (1965). *The history of education: Educational practice and progress considered as a phase of the development and spread of Western civilization*. Boston: Houghton Mifflin. (Original work published 1920)

Derman-Sparks, L. (1993). *Anti-bias curriculum: Tools for empowering young children*. Washington, DC: National Association for the Education of Young Children.

Dillard, J. (1972). *Black English: Its history and usage in the United States*. New York: Random House.

Hanson, M. (1998). Ethnic, cultural, and language diversity in intervention settings. In E. Lynch & M. Hanson (Eds.), *Developing cross-cultural competence* (2nd ed.). Baltimore: Paul H. Brookes.

Joe, J., & Malach, R. (1998). Families with Native American roots. In E. Lynch & M. Hanson (Eds.), *Developing cross-cultural competence* (2nd ed.). Baltimore: Paul H. Brookes.

Krogh, S. (1994). *Educating young children: Infancy to grade three*. New York: McGraw-Hill.

Ramsey, P. (1987). *Teaching and learning in a diverse world: Multicultural education for young children*. New York: Teachers College Press.

Swiniarski, L., Breitborde, M., & Murphy, J. (1999). *Educating the global village: Including the young child in the world*. Upper Saddle River, NJ: Merrill.

Takaki, R. (1993). *A different mirror*. Boston: Little, Brown.

Willis, W. (1998). Families with African American roots. In E. Lynch & M. Hanson (Eds.), *Developing cross-cultural competence* (2nd ed.). Baltimore: Paul H. Brookes.

York, S. (1991). *Roots and wings*. St. Paul, MN: Redleaf Press.

Zuniga, M. (1998). Families with Latino roots. In E. Lynch & M. Hanson (Eds.), *Developing cross-cultural competence* (2nd ed.). Baltimore: Paul H. Brookes.

5

PERSPECTIVES ON TODAY: CURRENT ISSUES

In an educational experience that is truly shared, choices and decisions have to be made with the widest possible consensus, and with a deep respect for a plurality of ideas and viewpoints.

Sergio Spaggiari

▼ Chapter Objectives

After reading this chapter, you should be able to:

▼ Describe the varying views of some of today's more perplexing issues related to young children and their education.

▼ View your own education program in the context of various approaches to teacher education.

As you think about and apply chapter content on your own, you should be able to:

▼ Analyze each of the chapter's issues in greater depth.

▼ Add issues of your own to discussions of early childhood and perhaps, research them more fully.

▼ Take your own stand on the issues and add this thinking to your growing philosophy of early education; consider writing a first-draft philosophy statement.

Numerous and complex issues face today's early childhood professionals. All of these issues reflect the society we now live in and all will affect you in some way as you enter the world of teaching. This chapter presents several of these. Some issues, such as more or less structure in curriculum and instruction, relate directly to the curriculum and the planning that goes into it. Others, such as schooling from what age, might not have such a direct impact on everyday teaching but could change the quality and quantity of available resources or influence the knowledge children bring with them to their learning experiences.

The issues presented here are frequently the subject of research, opinion writing, position papers, and legislative action. Rarely is there agreement on all sides as to the best course of action for resolving the various views on how to solve problems. Decisions are often made for political or financial reasons or because of convenience, perceived needs of children, or preferred philosophies. This last reason is one you might try as an approach to finding your own conclusions as you read about each issue.

To think philosophically, try turning back to chapter 2 and reading again the varying ways of looking at early development and education. Then, as you consider each of the issues, think how you might respond from each of the theoretical points of view. Such an exercise might not only help you see how to deal with issues in your own future classroom but may lead you toward the development of a more fully realized philosophy of early education.

As the varying sides of each issue are presented, we include expert opinions for you to contemplate as well as examples of research. At times the research focuses on toddlers or preschoolers and at other times on children in the primary grades. These are only samples of available studies, and we encourage you to expand your knowledge through your own library research.

ISSUE 1: SCHOOLING FROM WHAT AGE?

School-entry age is an issue peculiar to educators involved in the early years. It is one that has given rise to philosophical and practical arguments over many centuries, with the most recent battle having begun some four decades ago with the onset of Head Start. As you read in chapter 3, it was believed by many at the time that children from economically disadvantaged families might well benefit from earlier entry into formal school learning. It was during this time, as well, that middle-class U.S. society seemed increasingly inclined to push children to be more competitive in academics and after-school activities. For the youngest children, even infants, rote learning of letters and corresponding sounds became popular with some eager parents. In many schools both public and private, elementary curriculum was watered down for kindergarten use and upper-grade material was similarly watered down for the primary grades. Thus, for a while in the 1960s and 1970s, encouraging young children of all classes and abilities to make the most of themselves and to speed their growth toward maturity was a national theme.

During this era, many professionals and parents who chose not to push their children expressed concerns. One of the best known publications of the time was *Better Late Than Early*, by Raymond Moore and Dorothy Moore (1975). Agreeing that early care and education might be advantageous for the children of working parents or for those with special needs, the Moores argued, however, that the home should be the primary institution for young children, that preschool probably is not needed for the larger population, that effective government-run preschool programs would be too costly to maintain well, and that planners of programs for younger children might well move too far too fast, with little or no regard to what research could tell them.

Even more widely read was David Elkind's (1981) *The Hurried Child*, a book that provided eloquently quotable arguments against the push to have young children learn more quickly and grow up faster. Elkind pointed with concern not only to pressured academics but to summer camps that were moving from traditional outdoor sports and campfire routines to specialized training in foreign languages, computers, tennis, and so on. Then there was the growing need for increasing numbers of children to travel back and forth alone between their divorced parents. Meanwhile, the many forms of media were beginning to present precociously sexual images of young children, and adult clothing styles were being sold for all ages, even preschoolers. Commenting on all these pressures, Elkind noted that:

> in middle-class America . . . [c]hildren have to achieve success early or they are regarded as losers. It has gone so far that many parents refuse to have their children repeat or be retained in kindergarten—despite all the evidence that this is the best possible time to retain a child. "But," the parents say, "how can we tell our friends that our son failed kindergarten?" (p. 17)

For those who were concerned about pressuring young children academically, psychologically, and socially, early childhood education was anything but a panacea for U.S. society. It would be far better, many argued, to avoid putting children in school as long as possible. The Moores (1975), for example, argued that 8 years old is plenty early and that some children should wait until they are 10 or even 12.

In recent years, a third view on when children should enter school has arisen: essentially, if and when they choose to (or their parents choose for them). Some parents have decided to educate their youngsters entirely at home. Of course, home schooling, especially for younger children, is historically quite commonplace. Yet, the move toward school-based early education has been so pervasive in recent decades that a parental decision to educate children at home has become noteworthy. Two basic motivations have been responsible for the growth of home-schooling: parents' belief that they can do a better job of teaching than schools can, and the desire to transmit family religious values within the context of the children's education (Galen & Pitman, 1991). The attitudes of state legislatures, departments of education, local school districts, and the general public toward home schooling vary from state to state and across time. In some states and districts, parents need only register with a superintendent's office; in others they might be required to hold valid teaching certificates. Clearly, the status of home schooling is in transition. Because its popularity is relatively recent, there is as yet little research pro-

Should children enroll in education experiences from an early age, or is their growth better fostered by remaining at home? Experts disagree.

viding definitive information that tells what is required to make home schooling successful.

We are left, then, with questions: When is the right time to begin a child's formal, school-based education? Is there ever a best time? In the next sections we look at each alternative more closely and then pause to consider our individual responses.

Early School Experiences Give Children More Benefits

The 1990s were marked by a great increase in knowledge about the importance of the earliest years in children's lives. Biological and psychological research continually uncovered new data pointing to the influence that environment and experience have on cognitive, social, emotional, and physical development. Early experiences were also found to have a profound influence on later life and the effects of early experiential deprivations difficult to rectify later.

With these findings firmly in mind, many began to argue for more opportunities for early—and earlier—education. They often referred to "optimal early education and care" as a "birthright of every child" that would ensure that all children:

- Develop a sense of emotional security.
- Have physical needs for nutrition and health met.
- Experience a wide variety of sensory and cognitive experiences.
- Develop social skills outside the family circle. (Seefeldt, 1990)

During the same decade, the increasing popularity and understanding of the ideas of Lev Vygotsky suggested a need for peer interaction beyond the confines of the home. As you read in chapter 2, the Vygotskian view stresses the importance of social interaction in the growth of cognition. This is a prime argument in favor of the proponents of earlier educational experiences.

We can point, as well, to research showing what can be accomplished by early experiences, particularly for children experiencing various deprivations. Alice Honig (1990) cited a study in which 13 orphaned babies, whose cognitive skills appeared delayed, were paired with institutionalized women with cognitive disabilities. These women, as well as the institution's matrons, gave the babies constant attention and encouragement in their development, and they were all subsequently adopted. One or 2 years later, the mean IQs of the adopted babies had increased more than 30 points, whereas infants still at the orphanage who had not received the extra attention lost an average of 26 points. A follow-up study 30 years later showed the gains to have been maintained and the "graduates" of the experimental group to be far more productive citizens than those who had not received special treatment or been adopted. A second study, the Carolina Abecedarian Project (1999), provided quality child care and educational activities for 57 children from infancy through age 5; another 54 were placed in a nontreated control group. The 57 were provided with games that focused on social, emotional, and cognitive development, particularly pertaining to language. Although the intervention terminated when they entered school, the children in the treatment group had higher average scores on mental tests throughout their teen years. As young adults they continued to show enhanced cognitive skills in both reading and mathematics. In addition, they were more likely to be in college, older when their first child was born, and more likely to be employed as compared to their peers who did not attend preschool.

In general, research on the advantages of early education is focused on children at risk, as was the case in both studies just described. To proponents of this view, however, it is a small stretch of common-sense reasoning to realize that any child can benefit from a quality experience in an educational setting. No family should be expected to supply every benefit a youngster needs to achieve optimum success in development. As Honig (1990) concluded, "From the earliest cradle days, small persons known as infants are entitled to the highest-quality education that parents and caregivers in partnership can provide" (p. 97).

Children Benefit More From Remaining at Home Longer

The same biological and psychological research from the 1990s has been used by those who believe that schooling is better delayed than rushed:

> So sensitive are these first years of life to environmental conditions, it is argued, that only the parents, within the security of the home, should educate the young. Providing early care and education is not only the parents' responsibility, but early separation of parents and child could be detrimental. (Seefeldt, 1990, pp. 58–59)

It can be pointed out that youngsters in a school setting must share the teacher's attention, follow rigid schedules, and get along with many other children—a difficult task in the early stages of social development.

Today, a large percentage of children have been observed failing kindergarten and must repeat or be placed in a *transitional* class for another year. The feelings of failure and stress on these children and their families may well be one reason that kindergarten failure is a strong predictor of high school dropout. If children were not so hurried into the school setting, they would have longer to build their confidence, self-esteem, and cognitive readiness for the experience. Of particular concern are boys, whose maturity frequently lags behind girls', thus making them more likely to be designated as academically at risk and placed in compensatory programs.

Raymond Moore and Dennis Moore (1990) argue strongly for the advantages of keeping children at home in the early years unless there is an important reason, such as major developmental delays, to provide them with outside help. They take issue with the research showing the great benefits of Head Start, pointing out that such studies were focused on graduates of highly acclaimed, well-funded programs. More run-of-the-mill settings, they maintain, would probably not demonstrate similar findings. Nevertheless, the research has been used successfully to convince the U.S. Congress to fund a nationwide network of sites that could not possibly equal the quality of those in the studies. Additionally, the Moores object to using the same studies of children with various disadvantages to argue for all children. "This is much like saying that if hospitals help ill children, all healthy youngsters should be hospitalized, too" (p. 123).

The Moores (1990) also can point to research showing the negative results of providing education too early. For example, in one wealthy school district in Michigan, extra funding was provided for early admission to kindergarten. Entry was competitive, based on readiness tests. The experiment lasted 14 years, after which it was found that:

- Nearly one third of the children became "poorly adjusted."
- Only about 1 in 20 became outstanding in leadership.
- Nearly 3 of 4 children actually lacked leadership skills.
- About 1 in 4 of these highly capable children performed at below-average academic level or had to repeat a grade.
- For many of the children, the experience was one of personal failure, destructive of self-respect. (p. 127)

The Moores (1990) also described research from New Jersey in which 500 children from kindergarten through high school were studied. It was found that children who were bright but young when they began school "did not realize their potential. They tended also to be physically less mature, emotionally less stable, and less likely to exercise leadership than those who were not rushed" (p. 128).

It is the contention of the Moores that studies such as these two point out the need for children to enter schools at later, rather than earlier, times in their lives. A most appropriate age would be 7 or 8, and some children might even wait until they are 12. Such a delay would not only provide time for children to mature sufficiently so that the rigors of institutionally scheduled days would be undaunting but also let parents determine how ready their children were to read, write, and learn mathematical processes. Surely, in times as stressful as ours, young children deserve to be sheltered long enough to prepare them for the years to come.

What Do You Think?

Although you are most likely in training to become a teacher in a school or center, it is important to consider positions taken by those on all sides of this argument. You may, in fact, find yourself in conversation or negotiations with home-schooling parents. What do you think are the positive points and the dangers of early education? Of staying home longer?

ISSUE 2: TOGETHER OR APART? THE BEST PLACEMENT OF CHILDREN WITH SPECIAL NEEDS

As you are aware, this entire series of books is dedicated to the concept of early childhood education for all children, those who are developing typically and atypically alike. The authors agree with the Division for Early Childhood (DEC) of the Council for Exception Children (CEC) that there should exist "full and successful access

Are youngsters with special needs better served in settings designed just for them or in inclusion sites?

to health, social service, education, and other supports and services for [all] young children and their families that promote full participation in community life" (1996, p. 1). For the authors, there is not a dichotomy between regular children and special children; rather, the vision is one of a continuum along which many levels of development and across which several types of development occur. Having said that, it should not be assumed that we also have a single vision of how and where all children are best served educationally.

For more than three decades, debates among the experts have occurred in legislatures, courtrooms, classrooms, conferences, and professional journals on just this subject. The first impetus for debate was the 1968 requirement that at least 10% of Head Start enrollees be children with disabilities. The next, and more widely influential, event occurred 7 years later when the United States Congress passed Public Law 94–142 which gave all children the opportunity to be educated in the environment "least restrictive" to their learning. It remained for educators, psychologists, doctors, and at times judges and juries to determine what least restrictive meant for each child or group of children.

At that point, research on the topic was in its infancy, because including children with disabilities in regular classrooms was not yet common. Reauthorization of the 1975 law occurred in 1990, and it was given a new name that remains today: the Individuals with Disabilities Education Act (IDEA). In 1997, the least restrictive environment provisions were strengthened to include emphasis on incorporating children with special needs into the regular curriculum. By the 1990s, a history of research had been building, and placements could be made more knowledgeably. However, the debate continued, because the variables were so many and so complex and the findings sometimes conflicted. In addition, each state was free to interpret the law as it saw fit, leading to different rules and guidelines as well as to widely varying levels of funding. The result has been that there is no consistency of treatment for young children throughout the U.S. or between communities or different kinds of sites.

It appears that passage of laws, decades of research, and the best of intentions still leave room for debate. Today, fewer people are likely to argue that either inclusion or segregation should be total; rather, the dichotomy is more likely to be found between those who feel that all children should be served in regular classrooms unless there is good reason not to and those who prefer pull-out programs of specialized instruction unless there is good reason for inclusion. You are now invited to join the debate as we consider the problems and opportunities of educating all young children together—or apart.

Inclusion Is Preferred for Most Young Children With Special Needs

Legal requirements over the past decades indicate a need for choosing inclusion over separation whenever feasible. IDEA legislation and its predecessors place this responsibility squarely on the shoulders of the U.S. education establishment. As important as the passage of any law, however, is the thinking that led to it. Most observers of the history of special education point to three traditional foundations: moral, rational, and empirical (Bailey, McWilliam, Buysse, & Wesley, 1998).

The moral argument is simply that children with disabilities have the right to experience the same fullness of life, including education, that typically developing children do. Thus, systematic segregation of children with special needs becomes as immoral as systematic segregation based on race or economic class.

Rational arguments are those that suggest policies that will logically benefit children in the typically developing group as well as those with delays or disabilities. It might be asserted then, that including children with disabilities in a general classroom can provide them a more challenging learning environment, opportunities to observe and learn from more competent peers, real-life contexts for learning skills, and a more socially responsive and facilitative environment (Bricker, 1995). In addition, young children have yet to develop biases against particular groups of people and will be more accepting of differences, early acceptance will most likely lead to later acceptance as well, and early placement should lead teachers and parents to assume in subsequent years that inclusion is the norm (Buysse & Bailey, 1993). Advantages for the typically developing children might include helping them appreciate individual differences, become more accepting of people with disabilities, and even become more accepting of their own strengths and weaknesses.

Empirical arguments for inclusion relate to the research that has occurred over the past decades. Studies at the elementary school level have been largely positive whereas those done in preschools are even more so (Bailey et al., 1998). For example, a major review of research found that social competence was generally enhanced for children with special needs in regular classroom settings, often because they had more social interactions there than in a segregated classroom. Having a larger percentage of typically developing children in a class was also found to be beneficial. In one study of children with visual impairments, those in inclusive settings "engaged in more social interaction, less unoccupied play, and less inappropriate or self abusive behavior than similar children in segregated classes" (Odom & Diamond, 1998, p. 10).

Moral, rational, and empirical arguments, then, appear to favor the concept of inclusion for young children with special needs.

Problems With Inclusion

The rhetoric of inclusion may create unrealistic expectations while ignoring the very real needs of many children, according to a good number of special educators, legislators, and parents of children with developmental delays and disabilities. According to this view, the assumption that widespread inclusion will bring with it a host of positive outcomes might well be naive, is not based on sufficient research, and is focused on conceptual notions rather than on practical applications.

In the decades since passage of the first special education laws, advocacy has concerned itself primarily with placement in programs rather than on the needs of individual children and the goals of their families (Bricker, 1995). Such misplaced focus has led to, and will continue to lead to, any number of potential problems. For example, "parents may feel forced to place their children in settings they might not otherwise select" (Bricker, 1995, p. 182). It could be that the parents may have very legitimate reasons for desiring that their children be in segregated settings: more qualified teachers, better quality and more intense services, or increased probability of placing the children in a regular classroom the following year.

Another potential problem is the loss of control of resources as well as the loss of the resources themselves. As more and more children with special needs are incorporated into the general education system, there may be a perceived need for fewer professional advocates and other resources. One writer asks, "Without maintaining a presence at the decision-makers' table, do we run the risk of seeing hard-won resources dwindle away or being reallocated to non-disabled children?" (Bricker, 1995, p. 187).

A third concern is the amount of training that teachers and aides receive for working with young children with special needs. The variety of disabilities is such that many or most of these children need access to specialists, at least during the early years, and a very small number of generalists are prepared with such skills. Furthermore, the necessary training is extensive enough to be less than attractive to professionals whose salaries do not reflect their expertise.

In addition to teacher training, necessary alterations and adaptations to the environment may present costs that school districts are unable or unwilling to support. One writer describes the first-day experiences of a young girl in a wheelchair entering her classroom with initial enthusiasm (Sheldon, 1996). She soon discovers, however, that she can't reach the paint at the easel and her wheelchair won't fit into the dramatic play area. When she tries to move into other sections of the room she accidently knocks toys from their shelves. There are no puzzles with large enough pieces for her to manipulate, the sensory table is too high to reach, and circle time is an exercise in frustration because there is no good place for her to sit and participate. Although a few alterations might make the environment more hospitable to this child, others would be expensive and difficult. In addition, the teacher may not be willing to alter an entire classroom for a single child. If other children with special needs were also added to this classroom, there could be even more complex environmental issues.

It has been pointed out that teachers face continual pressures to raise their children's test scores while teaching larger classes, covering more content, and being provided with insufficient planning time (Winter, 1997). Adding the need to plan curriculum and alter the environment for a single child or a small number of children, each of whom takes more time and effort than typically developing children, is an extra burden.

Research has not shown that young children with special needs who are placed in regular classrooms make significant gains in language or other cognitive areas (Hundert, Mahoney, Mundy, & Vernon, 1998). Studies of social interactions have demonstrated more complex results. Generally, youngsters with mild to moderate disabilities make social progress in a regular classroom whereas those with severe disabilities progress better with the more directive approaches provided in segregated settings (Buysse & Bailey, 1993).

Writers who note these results are careful to add that their findings may not argue for a return to more segregated days. Instead, they caution against a wholesale acceptance of inclusion without consideration of program quality, supportive resources, teacher education, individual children's needs, and continued research designed to get at the complexity of issues faced by special educators.

What Do You Think?

Is the concept of full inclusion, or much greater inclusion, too idealistic? Or is segregation unfair to young children? Should we jump into more classroom inclusion and figure things out as we go? Or should we be more cautious and await the results of continued research? What decisions are most fair to children and their teachers and parents?

ISSUE 3: THE VIOLENCE THAT PERVADES TODAY'S CULTURE

Although the United States has not been involved in military conflict on its own territory for a very long time, our culture as a whole is increasingly a violent one, with repercussions for even the very youngest of our citizens. At least some of the blame can be traced directly to the powerful influence of television and to the products that are marketed in conjunction with violent child-oriented programs.

One researcher in this field pointed out that "aggression is largely a learned behavior, and television is one of the teachers" (Boyatzis, 1997, p. 75). Quite significantly, more than 30 years of research have verified that television promotes aggression in young children for several reasons: observation of real-life aggression leads to increased aggressiveness in behavior; observation of TV aggression leads to desensitization toward and acceptance of violence in real life; the more children see violence on TV, the more likely they are to imitate it, particularly in their dramatic play; and, finally, violent TV provides young children with "scripts" that they then use both in their dramatic play and in real-life interactions (Boyatzis, 1997; National Association for the Education of Young Children [NAEYC], 1990).

Despite the findings of this research, the amount of violence shown to young children on TV shows has increased since the mid-1980s, when the federal government deregulated the medium. For example, a major concern for many preschool teachers in the early to mid-1990s, was the popularity of *The Mighty Morphin Power Rangers*. Traditionally, a single children's cartoon program might have had 20 to 25 acts of violence, although such acts in another popular show, *Ninja Turtles* were counted at close to 100. Those numbers were certainly high enough to cause concern, but *Mighty Morphin Power Rangers* outdid them all, with more than 200 acts of violence per show (Boyatzis, 1997; Levin & Carlsson-Paige, 1995). Although such statistical research was largely focused on the programs just described, other shows that rise and fall in popularity over time often present the same problem.

If television were the only villain promoting a culture of violence, a concerted nationwide effort might actually wipe out the problem. The situation becomes more complex, however, when the influence of movies, computer games, videos, and an increasingly diverse collection of toy weapons is considered. Add to all these observations of the wider culture, where statistics demonstrate that a view of American society as violent is not just in the imagination. For example, the murder rate in this country is 10 times that of England and 25 times that of Spain. Or, to take just one large city, a study of children in Chicago found that 74% had observed at least one violent crime and 46% had actually experienced at least one. Studies in other cities have found similar results (Wallach, 1993). Some of the causes of our violent society have been listed as "poverty, racism, unemployment, illegal drugs, inadequate or abusive parenting practices, and real-life adult models of violent problem-solving behavior" (NAEYC, 1990, p. 18), but any number of other countries have similar difficulties multiplied many times over, without the same violence levels. It is, perhaps, the young children who suffer most; at the time of their lives when they are most in need of protection, security, and safety, they are bombarded with the anxiety, threat, and insecurity inherent in the violence of the culture around them.

What can teachers of young children do? Much has been written about the problem of young children in a violent society, particularly as reflected in increasingly violent behaviors in early childhood centers and classrooms. Most researchers are in agreement that there is no single, best solution, but experts tend to favor either total abolition of violent dramatic play in the classroom or acceptance of it within limits. Here are their views and supporting arguments.

Aggression of All Sorts Should Be Abolished in Centers and Classrooms

One writer argues that for at least a few hours each day children should "not be subjected to chaos, confusion, and wild, aggressive play" and that if teachers permit such play, they are sending children a message that "powerful positions are important, and if you make a lot of noise and disrupt the work of a lot of people, you are more important, because you get more attention" (Kuykendall, 1995, p. 58). This long-time director of early education programs also points out that children can work out their feelings in activity centers such as those related to construction or art; that there is often little time for teachers to sit down and sufficiently discuss the negative aspects of aggressive play; that young children often confuse fantasy and reality, leading to unfortunate behaviors; and that nonaggressive children may actually be inspired by their more aggressive playmates to imitate their behavior.

Echoing Kuykendall's views, Beverly Jackson (1997), who has studied the impact of violence on infants and toddlers, concluded that early childhood professionals need to "provide a safe haven for children who have witnessed or experienced violence" (p. 68).

Aggressive Play Can Be Channeled in Positive and Beneficial Ways

At its best, say advocates of this view, such activities as war play help children "work on their understanding of the boundaries between pretend and reality, build basic cognitive concepts, develop a beginning understanding of political and moral ideas, and even learn about cooperation and the needs of others." Furthermore, such play "can serve as an important vehicle through which children can work on the thoughts and feelings they have about the violence they see around them" (Carlsson-Paige & Levin, 1990, p. 31).

One writer goes so far as to embrace violent TV characters saying, "I think we have a responsibility to work with this material, to teach our values through and around this stuff." Her argument is that she prefers the opportunity to "involve children in conversations about values and feelings" and that whether they are raised in safe environments or horrific ones, children are surrounded by frightening violence that can and should be dealt with in the classroom (Greenberg, 1995, p. 60).

What Do You Think?

The writers just cited are all experts in the field of early education, yet grappling with this difficult issue leads them to very different positions. You, too will need to decide how to deal with the violence that seems to seep into many U.S. centers and classrooms today. Do you think of your future center or classroom as a safe haven where no violence is permitted, or do you see it as a place where children can learn to work out their conflicts in a protected environment? Is there a middle road?

ISSUE 4: CULTURAL PLURALISM IN THE CLASSROOM AND CURRICULUM

The United States has always been a nation of immigrants, but in recent years, new and changing laws have ensured that the ethnic and cultural mix among those entering the country has grown more complex. Records kept from 1820 show that for 150 years the vast majority of immigrants came from European countries. Those who immigrated from this continent came primarily from Mexico and the Caribbean. Since 1970 however, Mexico has remained a major contributor of immigrants, but the Philippines, China, Korea, and Vietnam have taken over the earlier dominance of European countries (Garcia, 1994).

Such increasing complexity poses a number of problems for teachers and caregivers hoping to make their young newcomers feel welcome, comfortable, and competent in their efforts to learn English. For example, in Florida and California, where educators once assumed that a knowledge of Spanish was the single necessary linguistic tool, command of numerous languages from Haitian Creole to Korean would now be advantageous.

Another problem even more complicated than that of language learning pertains to the various views that are held about U.S. culture: the melting pot versus stew versus tossed salad concepts of what our culture is and should be. How we define our national "dish" will determine to a great extent the ways in which we define and introduce U.S. culture to children. It will also determine how we introduce majority-culture children to the many minority cultures represented within our schools and centers.

As educational institutions, parents, and legislatures struggle to define our increasingly complex culture and its meaning for education, subissues inevitably arise. Should there be multicultural education, or should there be an effort to bring everyone together in a traditionally defined U.S. unity? If there is multicultural education, should it emphasize the differences between cultures or the commonalities? Does self-esteem come to children when their cultures are studied and differentiated, or do they actually feel better when they sense that they are more part of the in-group? And what about the increasing numbers of children who come from mixed ethnicities and cultures? How should they define themselves?

Although in-depth studies of cultures may be most appropriate for children who have matured somewhat in their understanding of history and geography, the issues relating to multicultural education can not be avoided by early educators. For more than two decades, research has shown us that children observe and respond to racial cues well before their second birthday; are aware by preschool age that people may label other races positively or negatively; and soon afterward begin developing their own complex racial attitudes, which are generally solidified by the end of elementary school (Katz, 1976). Thus, the contentious discussion on the topic of multicultural education that has pervaded U.S. schools, magazines, TV shows, and legislative discussions in recent years has application to early childhood education from the toddler years on, and to families from infancy.

Given the need, then, to provide multicultural education in the preschool and primary years, it should be said that this education must do more than provide children with information about their own and other cultures. It must permeate classroom life in many ways. Teachers should be aware of their own cultural values as they choose books to read, create bulletin boards, and develop themes of study. They must be sure that they make all children feel welcome and valued just as they are and emphasize both respect and civility for all. Stacey York (1991) stated the value of multicultural education in the early years quite eloquently when she said that young children

Today's multi-cultural education must take into account such modern day commonplaces as transracial adoptions.

deserve to be in programs where it is safe for them to be who they are. Children deserve to know the truth about themselves, the real world, and the people in it. Children have the right to feel good about themselves, to learn to be courageous, and not to feel like victims. Children are entitled to their cultural heritage and to be proud of it. (p. 23)

York's statement would find little disagreement among those who advocate dealing with multicultural issues in the classroom, but the ways to go about doing so have long been a cause for argument. Following are three different views for you to consider.

There Should Be an Emphasis on Commonalities

There are those who feel that it is the job of schools to emphasize the commonalities among people in order to build a uniquely U.S. culture. This approach has worked in the past, they argue, and it should serve us well now and in the future despite the introduction of many new cultural and ethnic backgrounds to our schools and communities.

Arguing for this view, Diane Ravitch (1991), who writes about national issues in education, agrees that children need to learn about other cultures as well as their own. She also wrote, however, that "priority must be given to teaching about the history and culture of the United States . . . ," that the historic role of the schools "has been to help forge a national identity that all Americans share. And the increasing diversity of our population makes it even more imperative that our schools teach children what we as Americans have in common" (pp. 8–9).

Ravitch (1991) disagrees with the critics who say that her view "disparages the role and contributions of minority groups" (p. 8). The common culture she says, is "the work of whites and blacks, of men and women, of Native Americans and African Americans, of Hispanics and Asians . . . and millions of other individuals who added their voices to the American chorus" (p. 9).

There Should Be an Emphasis on Diversity

Those who prefer this approach to education believe strongly that it is a better way to increase children's self-esteem and appreciation of individual differences, while building toward a more just society. An awareness and appreciation of all the cultural groups represented in a school or center, and of the many groups outside it, is a more realistic way of dealing with the increasing complexity of U.S. society, they believe. Finally, they say that those who argue for a study of commonalities may well be fearful of change and nostalgic for a past that no longer exists.

"The United States has always been ambivalent about diversity" wrote Patricia Ramsey and Louise Derman-Sparks (1992), both leaders in multicultural education for young children. "Immigrants, welcomed by the words engraved on the Statue of Liberty, have often found themselves despised and rejected by bosses and teachers" (p. 10). To counteract this situation, they have spent many years developing and sharing with others an early childhood curriculum that is antibias, not simply multicultural but an active initiative against the holding of biases against any group.

> We must help all people recognize that, as long as some groups are excluded and alienated from educational and occupational opportunities, our world is precarious. In our work, we need to show how prejudice hurts all children—including European Americans—and that more open and just schools and social structures benefit everybody. (p. 11)

Agreeing with this point of view, three African-American early childhood professors (Boutte, LaPointe, & Davis, 1993) describe the discomfort many of their student teachers have in dealing with racial issues that come up in their school classrooms and their attempts to avoid discussions that would deal with the issues. These professors believe that "when we fail to acknowledge differences in individuals, we may send a message that differences are not appreciated or that they are negative" (p. 20).

There Should Be Emphasis on Individuals

Traditionally, the arguments over multicultural education have been primarily represented by the two opposing views of education just described. More recently, a third view has arisen that takes into account an increasingly common situation in which the children in any given classroom do not necessarily represent specifically definable groups. This view is an extension of the second one, in which uniqueness of racial and cultural groups is affirmed and studied. Now, however, individual differences are emphasized as well.

This third approach takes into account the fact that children of the same races or nationalities may have little else in common. Heritage, experience, social class, and linguistic backgrounds all contribute to the makeup of each child. In addition, the increasing numbers of transracial adoptions and multiracial children in U.S. classrooms may mean that the usual multicultural education, with its focus on group membership, may leave many children out.

Francis Wardle (1997) is a proponent of the view that multicultural education should not only emphasize antibias but also focus on individuals, rather than on groups. "The individual child exists within his/her own dynamic context, or milieu" says Wardle, and this "includes a variety of experiences that interact with each other to produce a unique environment" (p. 151). This educator believes that teachers should concentrate on individual children, creating an individualized multicultural program for each one. Only in this way, can we "allow each of our children to develop to their full potential" (p. 154).

What Do You Think?

Never before in our history have we had to contend with so many cultures, languages, and competing value systems as we do now. We cannot simply ignore these differences. They affect the children in our centers and classrooms, sometimes profoundly. You have read about three ways to view the situation in your teaching site. Does one of them seem superior to you? Why? Can you create a fourth of your own?

ISSUE 5: YOUNG CHILDREN IN A TECHNOLOGICAL AGE

The use of technology, in particular computers, by young children has become generally accepted by the educational community. It was not many years ago that the question of developmental appropriateness created a fierce debate among those who believed no age was too young to introduce children to the technology that was beginning to pervade most of society and those who feared the use of computers would deny children the access they need to hands-on manipulative materials. Each year it becomes more obvious that the former group is winning this argument on all fronts. As one educational researcher and writer concluded, "This is a question we should stop asking . . . computer use with children in early childhood has been shown to have a major, positive impact on social, emotional, language, and cognitive development" (Shade, 1996a, p. 43).

In fact, the National Association for the Education of Young Children (NAEYC, 1996) formally adopted a position statement regarding technology that demonstrates this evolution of opinion:

> The potential benefits of technology for young children's learning and development are well documented. . . . the research indicates that, in practice, computers supplement and do not replace highly valued early childhood activities and materials, such as art, blocks, sand, water, books, explorations with writing materials, and dramatic play. (p. 11)

The use of computers by even very young children has become accepted by most early educators. *How* they can best be used remains an issue.

In addition, the computer is increasingly viewed as a bridge between the physical and the abstract by "presenting concrete ideas in a symbolic medium" (Clements & Swaminathan, 1995, p. 27). Computer enthusiasts remind us that Piaget's concept of concrete operations did not refer merely to literal, three-dimensional concreteness but to what is meaningful to children. Thus, the computer becomes no less concrete than the long-popular, two dimensional book (Clements & Swaminathan, 1995; Shade, 1996a).

Now that most early childhood centers have at least one computer and the ratio of computers to children in elementary schools moves ever closer to the recommended 1:12 (Clements & Swaminathan, 1995), issues remain but are altered in focus. The curriculum and teaching methodology provided by an ever-expanding supply of software seem to fall into two competing groups. Read about them both and then decide what your own approach should be.

Computers Are Most Useful for Enhancing Skills

In its earliest days, the classroom computer was used largely for the purpose of skill enhancement. In the mid-1990s, software for tutorial purposes was still dominating the marketplace (Shade, 1996b). Software companies continue to promote large, comprehensive packages that include applications for such practice in both language arts and mathematics, providing teachers with ready-made, easy to use drills that require little teacher–child interaction time.

An additional attraction is that programming of this software requires little time, thus keeping costs low. Research has shown that this type of software can be useful in promoting reading readiness skills, including those that are most difficult for children to grasp. When computers are used for this purpose, the length of time children spend at the computer is important, since skill improvement is directly related to the time children are involved with the software (Clements & Swaminathan, 1995).

Using the Computer for Open-Ended Exploration

Drill-and-practice software provides children with the correct answers to their questions and problems. On the other hand, there is software that offers quite the opposite benefit, engaging children in creative play and open-ended problem solving. Although drill software is widely used to increase children's abilities in reading and math, some research (but not all) has shown that software with more room for creativity is actually more successful (Shade, 1996b).

Arguing for the more open-ended approach, the NAEYC *Position Statement* (1996) notes that such software enables the child "to find new challenges as she becomes more proficient. Appropriate visual and verbal prompts designed in the software expand play themes and opportunities while leaving the child in control" (p. 12).

A number of writers have observed that drill software tends to be associated with computers that have been placed in special labs rather than in classrooms. Those who favor open-ended software also prefer classroom-based hardware, believing that technology-based education is most effective when easily integrated into the ongoing curriculum and with everyday classroom materials.

What Do You Think?

Publishers and school systems have a long history of favoring the use of computer software that provides skill enhancement through drill and practice. This is the approach you may be more likely to encounter as you enter the teaching profession. Meanwhile, early childhood organizations such as the NAEYC and those who research the effects of computers on young children tend to favor more open-ended software. The costs of technology, although lessening over time, remain high for those on prescribed budgets (and that is, of course, most of us.) Thus, careful decisions about the type of software purchased must be made. Is there a direction that feels right to you? Finally, we have said that computers are generally accepted for early childhood, but this is not the case for everyone, as you saw in chapter 3 during a visit to the Waldorf school in Vancouver, British Columbia. Perhaps you are in agreement with this school's view, and there is no software at all that seems right to you.

ISSUE 6: MORE OR LESS STRUCTURE IN CURRICULUM AND INSTRUCTION?

In chapter 3 we described six rather different approaches to working with young children. Two of them (Head Start and corporate child care) might use any number of different curriculum and instruction formats depending on the philosophies of the particular sites. Two others (Montessori and Waldorf) approach their planning from a well-structured foundation. That is, materials and curriculum are fairly standard worldwide and teachers receive similar training in teaching methodology no matter where they study. The final two approaches (Reggio Emilia and the Project Approach) bring to the classroom a variety of curricular choices that emerge from interaction and negotiation among teachers and children. The resulting instruction leaves much to the children's direction, with support and guidance from the teachers as necessary and beneficial. Thus, these approaches can be described as less structured.

Because an approach to curriculum and instruction is *structured* does not mean that it doesn't take children's interests and needs into consideration. Maria Montessori and Rudolf Steiner both devoted time, thought, and energy to observing children in order to understand their interests, needs, and developmental patterns. Once they felt these were understood, curriculum and instruction were structured based on their observations.

In Montessori's case, for example, it was observations of children's preferences for meaningful experiences over the available toys that led her to take the children's experiences more seriously. She came to believe that for a period of the day, at any rate, the children preferred what adults would call work to more playful activities. Furthermore, the children did not simply role play their work; the experiences were real ones. In other words, there was no dramatic play area where children imitated their elders cleaning house. Rather, there were real brooms, mops, sponges, and soap, and the children applied themselves to keeping their classroom and its furnishings clean.

Conversely, it should be said that because an approach to curriculum and instruction is *unstructured* does not mean that it lacks planning. Rather, planning tends to be ongoing, flexible, and open to change. One might say, in fact, that more planning is actually necessary in an unstructured approach, because curriculum and materials are not provided in advance.

One typical method for initial planning is to make a *curriculum web*. In the project approach, this might be stream of consciousness thinking that results in a variety of topic-related words laid down as spokes radiating from the middle. These are then pared down to more manageable size, achieving increasing focus as planning progresses. Thus, planning in the project approach or in any other less-structured method is most definitely not linear. You are unlikely to witness a traditional lesson plan with its lists of objectives, procedures, materials, and evaluation activities. This type of lesson plan could certainly be created in an unstructured classroom, but only after an activity was completed.

Perhaps another way to describe structured and unstructured curriculum and instruction would be to call them *preplanned* and *planned-in-progress*. Each view has its strengths and each one, without continual oversight, could be carried too far. The preplanned and more structured approach could become "enbalmed," as each year the teacher returns to her collection of materials, "brings it all out and dusts it off and is ready to roll. It is, after all, new to *them*; they're not being shortchanged by her short-cuts. That she may be shortchanging herself only occasionally crosses her mind" (Jones & Nimmo, 1994, p. 77). The less-structured approach has its own dangers, those of becoming an "accidental/unidentified" curriculum, one that just happens and that no one names. Rather than being fully developed from children's observed interests and needs, "it's full of starting points for an emergent curriculum, but the teaching staff isn't about to put in extra time and energy. . . . They're content just to hang out with kids" (Jones & Nimmo, 1994, p. 77).

Each approach, then, has its inherent dangers, but each also has its strengths. The next two sections consider these more fully.

More Structure Is Better

In general, there are two basic ways we can look at more-structured curriculum and instruction. In the previous section, we described the first way, in which what happens in the classroom is determined by a particular theory or philosophy. Montessori and Steiner, for example, did not just philosophize and leave the practical follow-up to inter-pretation or mere chance. Instead, they worked to see that their thinking was reflected in actual classroom materials and activities. An advantage of a structured approach is that teachers, who have studied it extensively and been certified, know why they make curricular and instructional decisions. When difficulties of any sort arise, they have a well-articulated foundation of knowledge for making improvements. Their vision of the child is more or less clear, and they can create solutions to foster maximum develop-ment. In addition, for most of the solutions there are materials readily available or, at the least, a philosophy as to how those materials should be created for optimal learning.

A second view of a structured curriculum and instructional methodology is based on the perceived needs of a specific school, school system, or locality. One is most likely to encounter this view in a public school district or single school that has decid-ed to adopt a particular prepackaged curriculum. Oftentimes, the district or school reviews a variety of programs and then chooses one that seems to meet its needs; less often, a program is tailor-made under contract. Frequently, these structured programs are accompanied by some form of in-house teacher training as well as ongoing vis-its from programmatic experts and evaluation systems to monitor progress.

One notable example (Lemann, 1998) can be found in New York City, where a small collection of elementary schools were placed on the state's "registration review" list, designating them as at risk of being shut down due to persistent low stu-dent performance. Several approaches and prepackaged curricula were tried with varying results. Eventually, a reading curriculum called Success for All was adopted. This highly directive and prescriptive program is used in more than 1,000 schools across the United States. Its effectiveness is documented by large-scale comparisons of test scores in schools that use the program and similar ones that don't.

Teachers in Success for All schools are taught a complete set of techniques from specific catch phrases to specific hand signals. Through kindergarten and first grade, every single piece of teaching material is supplied by the program. What Success for All lacks in autonomy for teachers and creativity for children it makes up for with attention to detail and follow-through to ensure that every child actually learns to read. The result for the designated New York schools was that reading scores began to climb impressively, leading to their removal from the registration review list.

It is success stories such as these that provide arguments against the less-structured arrangements that have apparently led to widespread failure for many children in some schools. Yet, there are arguments to be made on behalf of less structure as well.

Less Structure Is Better

Approaches to curriculum that eschew a preplanned structure are frequently referred to as *emergent*. That is, what is studied emerges from the interests of children and teachers. These interests are not those of brief duration such as, perhaps, momentary excitement over a child's pet brought to school one day, but interests that are widespread and that seem to persist. It may be that the children as a group are aware of an interest and bring it up for discussion. At other times, the teacher may notice an interest or need that the children don't or have an interest of his or her own that could take the children into a new area of knowledge. In either case, the decision to pursue a study in depth becomes the result of negotiation among the children as well as between children and teacher. The teacher's responsibility, once a prospective study is defined, is to ensure that any required learning standards are successfully incorporated into the project or dealt with in other parts of the day as well as to be aware of implications for family and community values.

An advantage of this kind of approach is that it builds on the natural curiosity and enthusiasm of children. A love of learning may be the long-term result. In addition, skills are learned as they are needed for real-life situations. They are not provided to children in out-of-context drills that have little or no meaning. Thus, if a project requires knowledge not designated in the school district's plan for the age of a particular class, it may be that the children will move far ahead in that area.

Sometimes, community or social awareness grows beyond what would be expected of a particular age group. One such example is provided by a teacher of 4-year-olds in Seattle, Washington. On the way back from a library visit, her children asked about a sign for wheelchair-accessible parking next to a church they passed. She permitted them an exploratory detour, which led the youngsters to the discovery of the church's ramp entrance. In a follow-up discussion of the experience, the class expressed concern that their school had "too many stairs" and that one child's stepfather could never visit their class because he used a wheelchair. The teacher described her responsibilities in such a situation as "listening attentively to the children; watching them for cues about their interests, skills, questions, and knowledge . . . ; and introducing ideas, initiating exploration, and leading the children into new territory" (Pelo, 1997, p. 58).

The children eventually determined that they would try to make a ramp with parental help. The teacher created a planning web, communicated a number of times with parents, and stocked the classroom with various props to provide the children with the construction skills they would need. These included building materials, nuts and bolts, ramp-shaped blocks, and books about construction and people who use wheelchairs. Classroom activities included placing a doll in a small wheelchair to research the wheelchair accessibility of the classroom. Corrective rearrangements of the furniture were then made. In the end, the teacher felt as though she had failed in some respects because the proposed ramp proved too costly to build.

Such a "failure" is a very possible outcome of curriculum that pertains to real life. Learning that such failures take place is, of course, part of the knowledge that children gain from such projects.

What Do You Think?

As you have seen, both approaches to curriculum and instruction have their strengths and potential problems. Both engender learning in children, but the learning may be quite different from one setting to the next. In addition, more or less structure may work differently for different groups of children or for the preferences of different cultures. It is your turn now to think about what sorts of learning you value most and the kind of planning and teaching that best fits your own philosophy.

ISSUE 7: EDUCATING THE EDUCATORS OF YOUNG CHILDREN

How much, and what kind of, education and training do beginning teachers of young children need? Any attempt to answer this question leads directly to an intimately related second one: What, exactly, do we want children's learning experiences to be like? The answers to both questions have remained elusive for decades as legislatures, state departments of education, scholars, parents, and teachers themselves have debated them.

Whether you are enrolled in a community college, or 4-year undergraduate program, or postgraduate course, the decisions about what you study have been made for you, at least in part, by state regulations. What your state requires may be quite different from what any number of other states require, and there is a strong possibility that your state requirements are even now undergoing review with the probability of change.

The reasons for continuing disagreement about the appropriate education of young children and the training needed to prepare their teachers are many and varied and frequently subject to change. In general, these reasons reflect the evolution of our society and culture. One of the most important issues today pertains to professionalism.

What it means to be a *professional* can be defined in two general ways. In one instance, a professional is simply someone who makes a living at a particular occupation. In the other, a professional must have "a high degree of knowledge and skill developed over a lengthy period of preparation" (Spodek, 1991, p. 111). Traditionally, early childhood educators have been more likely to think of themselves along lines of the first definition and, indeed, legislation as well as pay scales in most states have done their best to validate this view. In recent years however, there has been a concerted effort on the part of organizations such as NAEYC and CEC/DEC to move everyone's perception from the first definition to the second.

One way to make the more stringent definition of *professional* a reality is to revisit our ideas of what constitutes an appropriate learning environment for young children. It is the position of the NAEYC and DEC, as well as of virtually all educational organizations, that early childhood settings are the most benign, receptive, and natural places for taking a proactive stance for the inclusive model of learning. It follows, then, that the teachers who work in these settings must be prepared to teach effectively across a greater variety of children than has traditionally been the case. It may well be that the extended education that these teachers need will lead to a greater regard for the field as a true profession. Nevertheless, controversy remains as the various issues pertaining to early childhood teacher education are considered. The thinking tends to fall into two general views.

All Early Childhood Teachers Should Be Thoroughly Educated in Both Regular and Special Education

Those who argue for this approach to teacher education also view child development as something that happens along a broad continuum, thus making a division between regular and special education inappropriate, especially for the younger preschool children. All teachers, they say, should have the knowledge and skills needed to handle the many levels of needs and abilities that children bring with them to their center or school. For example, the intrinsically motivated play-based curriculum that teachers of typically developing children specialize in and the teacher-directed individualized education required for children with special needs can be understood and used by teachers of all children. To segregate the two types of teacher education programs has even been called "immoral" and "inefficient" by one teacher educator who wrote:

> Such segregation practices in teacher training perpetuate the myth that particular types of children need teachers who have been trained in discrete bodies of knowledge and pedagogy accessible only to members of specialized fields of expertise. This kind of misguided educational decision making has led to second-class treatment of children whose development or social skills deviate from the ever narrowing norm. (Miller, 1992, p. 39)

Teacher Education Should Continue to Provide Specialists in Early Childhood Special Education

The proponents of this view do not argue that education students should only receive courses in one field or the other, but do make the case that the emphasis and specialized training need to be focused one way or the other. One writer who espoused this view believes that the need for all teachers to have a basic knowledge of special needs is "self-evident." However, she also wrote that there is a "need for continuing to have teachers who specialize in working with children with special needs. By merging teacher certifications, we risk minimizing the special challenges that some children face and that their parents, teachers, and therapists share as they support them" (VanArsdall, 1994, p. 90). She suggests that specialized courses in neuropsychology, language acquisition, and social–emotional development are necessary to serve children with special needs effectively. Without them, she said, "we do both children and teachers a disservice" (p. 90).

Those who espouse this view of teacher education also point to the practical fact that only a handful of states have mandated dual certification of early educators. For preservice teachers in all the other states, the longer, more intensive study required by a dually focused program would be requiring too much, particularly for a typically underpaid career.

What Do You Think?

If you are currently enrolled in an early childhood teacher education program, a decision about your own career and training may well have been made for you already. This decision may rest with your state's government or with the designers of the program you are in. There are other models however, in other places, determined by other governments and program designers. Consider the pros and cons of both views and the ways they are reflected in your own education: Given a choice, which approach do you prefer and why?

ISSUE 8: YOUNG CHILDREN IN THE 21ST CENTURY

This final section is shaped differently than the previous ones. Instead of asking you to consider conflicting sides of a single issue, it presents predictions for the new century, then leaves you to discuss their implications.

The first widely read author to predict the place of children and learning in the 21st century published his views 30 years before its beginning. In *Future Shock* (1970), *Learning for Tomorrow* (1974), and *The Third Wave* (1980), Alvin Toffler (1970) argued that the world was beginning to change so fast that all the traditional ways of learning and knowing would necessarily need to change as well. Education must be lifelong and its prime objective, he said, "must be to increase the individual's 'cope-ability'—the speed and economy with which he can adapt to continual change" (p. 403).

Three societal skills, Toffler (1970) said, would be necessary for survival, but each would present its own challenges: learning, relating, and choosing. As applied to the teacher's role, these three would include such considerations as:

- Today's facts become tomorrow's misinformation. So, children must learn how to discard old ideas and grasp new ones. They must, in other words, learn how to learn.

- With increased technology and change in all walks of life, relating to others will become a greater challenge. More imaginative grouping of children for learning may teach new lessons in making and maintaining rewarding human ties.

- Increasing options of all kinds present the increasing challenge of "overchoice." Children need to be taught what values are and how to define their own. Schools must stop shying away from teaching about values and embrace the subject.

Toffler's views and similar ones that followed his did not change education overnight, but they did open up an end-of-century debate that is represented in this chapter by the section More or Less Structure in Curriculum and Instruction.

In the 1990s, thinkers began to focus with increasing seriousness on the changes and continuities that the 21st century might bring and the kinds of people who could live most successfully in it. To a great extent, this thinking was influenced by the onset of just what Toffler predicted: a new, postindustrial, global, information age with its overlay of quickly expanding and radically changing technological capabilities. The qualities needed for success in the world of work, for example, are quite different than those historically valued. For example, one business writer (Pritchett, n.d.) suggested such practices as:

- Learning not to resist change while adapting—fast—to new ways of working.
- Working with a strong sense of urgency, emphasizing action.
- Accepting ambiguity and uncertainty.
- Becoming a lifelong learner.
- Managing one's own morale rather than expecting management to do it.
- Continuing to stretch oneself to be better than yesterday.

There is nothing in this list that would predict long-term stability in any aspect of one's work life. Instead, there is a predicted need to be flexible and ready for constant change. Another author, looking more holistically at the 21st-century mind that we all need to possess, suggests similar and complementary qualities (Sinetar, 1991). She wrote that our 21st-century minds will need to:

- Have a high tolerance for change, discontinuity, paradox.
- Be willing to think independently.
- Be nonentrenched and able to release unproductive beliefs.
- Be able to experiment, always willing to look for better ways to do things.

These are all qualities necessary for survival in a world that had begun to change with unprecedented speed well before the turn of the new century and shows few signs of slowing down. Not only will our world move faster in the new century, it will be more crowded as well. The United States Census Bureau shows a nation of approximately 275 million in the year 2,000, 323 million by 2020, and perhaps 394 million by midcentury. By that same midcentury, the U.S. population is projected to be 25% Black, Asian, or Native American, 25% Hispanic, and 50% Caucasian.

Children born at the turn of the century can expect to be about the same size as their parents, but life expectancy will continue to grow, to about 73 years for males and 80 years for females. Mortality rates for newborns, which in the 1990s were about 8 per 1,000, are predicted by the Center for Disease Control to fall dramatically, perhaps to as low as 1 per 1,000. Doctors will be able to cope more successfully with congenital defects and diseases, even before birth. Routine genetic screening should be able to identify risks to individual children, making treatment, family planning, and health advice individually applicable (Adler, 1998).

It appears that U.S. children in the 21st century may be healthier, more likely to survive disabling conditions, and more ethnically diverse. They will need skills to cope with constant change, the increasing incursion of technology, and the need to live harmoniously in ever more crowded conditions.

What Do You Think?

Consider the positions presented by thinkers of the late 20th century. Do you agree with them? What qualities would you add as being essential to the 21st-century citizen? Will these change for the children you teach? If so, how? What changes will, or should, there be in the education of early childhood teachers? In what ways can these teachers make their classrooms or centers more hospitable to children, taking into account the future you have identified?

EXTENDING YOUR LEARNING

1. Discover more controversial issues by interviewing teachers, center directors, principals, parents, school board members, and professors. Bring these, including arguments on various sides, to your class for discussion.

2. Research an issue—one discussed in this chapter or one you have discovered—through extended reading. Write a position paper that presents all sides as fairly and completely as possible, then presents your own opinion based on your reflections of what you have learned.

3. Stage a classroom debate around one or more issues discussed in this chapter. You can choose to follow the rules of formal debate or discuss more informally. You are encouraged to expand your reading and knowledge of the topic before you begin.

4. Be alert for newspaper articles, radio and TV broadcasts, and new magazine stories about the issues presented in this chapter, especially as related to early childhood. Keep a media journal for a month and then review the themes, issues, and trends you have collected.

5. Obtain a copy of the teacher certification standards for preschool and primary teachers in public schools in your state. Compare them to the requirements for a Child Development Associate or other types of training required for Head Start and childcare licensure.

6. Visit the NAEYC and DEC Web sites to explore the full text of position papers on inclusion, diversity, technology, and other issues.

7. Reflect back on your readings, class discussions, field experiences, and the notes you have kept after each chapter to create a philosophy of early education. Write a position statement that uses all this input as your basis. Consider this your first-draft thinking and, as you progress through your coursework and experiences with children, add to and delete as you deem appropriate. You might even save this paper for 5 years or more to see how your thinking changes and develops and to remind yourself of good ideas that might have been temporarily shelved.

INTERNET RESOURCES

Web sites provide much useful information for educators and we list some here that pertain to the topics covered in this chapter. The addresses of Web sites can also change, however, and new ones are continually added. Thus, this list should be considered as a first step in your acquisition of a larger and ever-changing collection.

American Montessori Society
www.amshq.org

Association Montessori Internationale
www.ami.edu

Early Childhood Education
www.ecewebguide.com

> Go to Anti-bias Resources
> www.ecewebguide.com/antibias.html

Educators for Social Responsibility
www.esnational.org

Head Start
www.acf.dhhs.gov/programs/hsb/

Home School Legal Defense Association
www.hslda.com

National Coalition on TV Violence
www.nctv.org

The Project Approach
www.ualberta.ca/

Reggio Emilia
www.cdacouncil.org/reggio-USA

References

Adler, J. (1998, November 2). Tomorrow's child. *Newsweek*, 54–65.
Bailey, D., McWilliam, R., Buysse, V., & Wesley, P. (1998). Inclusion in the context of competing values in early childhood education. *Early Childhood Research Quarterly, 13*(1), 27–47.

Boutte, G., LaPointe, S., & Davis, B. (1993). Racial issues in education: Real or imagined? *Young Children, 49*(1), 19–23.

Boyatzis, C. (1997). Of Power Rangers and V-Chips. *Young Children, 52*(7), 74–79.

Bricker, D. (1995). The challenge of inclusion. *Journal of Early Intervention, 19*(3), 179–194.

Buysse, V., & Bailey, D. (1993). Behavioral and developmental outcomes in young children with disabilities in integrated and segregated settings: A review of comparative studies. *The Journal of Special Education, 26*(4), 434–461.

Carlsson-Paige, N., & Levin, D. (1995). Can teachers resolve the war–play dilemma? *Young Children, 50*(5), 62–63.

Carlsson-Paige, N., & Levin, D. (1990). *Who's calling the shots?* Philadelphia: New Society.

Carolina Abecedarian Project, The. (1999). *Early learning, later success: The abecedarian study* [Online]. Available: http://www.fpg.unc.edu/~abc/embargoed/executive_summary.htm

Clements, F., & Swaminathan, S. (1995). Technology and school change: New lamps for old? *Childhood Education, 71*(5), 275–281.

Division for Early Childhood of the Council for Exceptional Children (1996). *Position on inclusion* [Online]. Available: www.dec-sped.org/positions/inclusio.html.

Elkind, D. (1981). *The hurried child: Growing up too fast too soon.* Reading, MA: Addison-Wesley.

Galen, J., & Pitman, M. (1991). *Home schooling: Political, historical, and pedagogical perspectives.* Norwood, NJ: Ablex.

Garcia, E. (1994). *Understanding and meeting the challenge of student cultural diversity.* Boston: Houghton Mifflin.

Greenberg, J. (1995). Making friends with the Power Rangers. *Young Children, 50*(5), 60–61.

Honig, A. (1990). Infant/toddler education issues: Practices, problems, and promises. In C. Seefeldt (Ed.), *Continuing issues in early childhood education.* Columbus, OH: Merrill.

Hundert, J., Mahoney, B., Mundy, F., & Vernon, M. (1998). A descriptive analysis of developmental and social gains of children with severe disabilities in segregated and inclusive preschools in southern Ontario. *Early Childhood Research Quarterly, 12*(1), 49–65.

Jackson, B. (1997). Creating a climate for healing in a violent society. *Young Children, 52*(7), 68–70.

Jones, E., & Nimmo, J. (1994). *Emergent Curriculum.* Washington, DC: National Association for the Education of Young Children.

Katz, P. (1976). The acquisition of racial attitudes in children. In *Towards the elimination of racism.* New York: Pergamon.

Kuykendall, J. (1995). Is gun play OK here??? *Young Children, 50*(5), 56–59.

Lemann, N. (1998). "Ready, read!" *The Atlantic Monthly, 282*(5), 92–104.

Levin, D., & Carlsson-Paige, N. (1995). The Mighty Morphin Power Rangers: Teachers voice concern. *Young Children, 50*(6), 67–72.

Miller, P. (1992). Segregated programs of teacher education in early childhood: Immoral and inefficient practice. *Topics in Early Childhood Special Education, 11*(4), 39–52.

Moore, R., & Moore, D. (1975). *Better late than early.* New York: Reader's Digest.

Moore, R., & Moore, D. (1990). When delay isn't procrastination. In C. Seefeldt (Ed.), *Continuing issues in early childhood education.* Columbus, OH: Merrill.

National Association for the Education of Young Children. (1990). NAEYC position statement on media violence in children's lives. *Young Children, 45*(5), 18–21.

National Association for the Education of Young Children. (1996). NAEYC position statement: Technology and young children—ages three through eight. *Young Children, 51*(6), 11–16.

Odom, S., & Diamond, K. (1998). Inclusion of young children with special needs in early childhood education: The research base. *Early Childhood Research Quarterly, 13*(1), 3–25.

Pelo, A. (1997). "Our school's not fair!" A story about emergent curriculum. *Young Children, 53*(1), 57–61.

Pritchett, P. (n.d.). *New work habits for a radically changing world.* Dallas: Pritchett & Associates.

Ramsey, P., & Derman-Sparks, L. (1992). Multicultural education reaffirmed. *Young Children, 48*(2), 10–11.

Ravitch, D. (1991). A culture in common. *Educational Leadership, 50*(2), 8–11.

Seefeldt, C. (1990). *Continuing issues in early childhood education*. Columbus, OH: Merrill.

Shade, D. (1996a). Are you ready to teach young children in the 21st century? *Early Childhood Education Journal, 24*(1), 43–44.

Shade, D. (1996b). Software evaluation. *Young Children, 51*(6), 17–22.

Sheldon, K. (1996). "Can I play too?" Adapting common classroom activities for young children with limited motor abilities. *Early Childhood Education Journal, 24*(2), 115–120.

Sinetar, M. (1991). *Developing a 21st century mind*. New York: Academic Press.

Spodek, B. (1991). Early childhood teacher training: Linking theory and practice. In S. Kagan (Ed.), *The care and education of America's young children: Obstacles and opportunities*. Chicago: University of Chicago Press.

Toffler, A. (1970). *Future shock*. New York: Random House.

Toffler, A. (1974). *Learning for tomorrow*. New York: Random House.

Toffler, A. (1980). *The third wave*. New York: Morrow.

VanArsdell, M. (1994). Preparing early childhood teachers for careers in learning. In S. Goffin & D. Day (Eds.), *New perspectives in early childhood teacher education: Bringing practitioners into the debate*. New York: Teachers College Press.

Wallach, L. (1993). Helping children cope with violence. *Young Children, 48*(4), 4–11.

Wardle, F. (1997). Proposal: An anti-bias and ecological model for multicultural education. In F. Schultz (Ed.), *Annual editions: Multicultural education*. Guilford, CT: Dushkin/McGraw-Hill.

Winter, S. (1997). "SMART" planning for inclusion. *Childhood Education, 73*(4), 212–218.

York, S. (1991). *Roots and wings*. St. Paul, MN: Redleaf Press.

Author Index